# PRESCRIPTION FOR SUCCESS:

## An Autobiography

## Marvin Nider

# PRESCRIPTION FOR SUCCESS:

## An Autobiography

ISBN-13: 978-0-9964460-7-5
ISBN-10: 0-9964460-7-9

Published by: Expert Author Publishing
http://expertauthorpublishing.com

Canadian Address:
1108 - 1155 The High Street,
Coquitlam, BC, Canada
V3B.7W4
Phone: (604) 941-3041
Fax: (604) 944-7993
US Address:

1300 Boblett Street
Unit A-218
Blaine, WA 98230
Phone: (866) 492-6623
Fax: (250) 493-6603

# Contents

# Chapter One
## A Little Place Called Cornwall, Ontario

I was born in the small, grey, sleepy, industrial city of Cornwall, Ontario. Famous for spawning several professional hockey players, bootleggers, and smugglers, it was also renowned for something else. As the home of several industries—cotton, paper, and Pioneer Chemicals—there was always "something in the air." Cornwall was famous primarily for being smelly.

This setting would seem to be an inauspicious way to start life, but growing up, I wasn't really aware of Cornwall's reputation. To me, it was a quiet and safe place to walk to school, ride bikes, and play around the canals along the St. Lawrence River. Because it was smaller, it didn't seem to have the same types of problems with teenagers getting into trouble that larger cities did. As a child, you aren't really aware of the greater world you live in anyway, just your own little universe with you and your family. I was mostly preoccupied with fighting off my big brother, who picked on me, engaging in my hobbies, and finding new ways to be enterprising.

The story of how I came into this world started when my father, who married quite late in life, finally found his match.

## Mom Meets Dad

My parents were not from Cornwall. My father, Oscar Niduvitch, was born in Ottawa, and my mother, Sarah Cohen, was born in Winnipeg. My mother was a very brave woman. She graduated from high school in 1944, and at eighteen she travelled by train to take a job in Ottawa. It was a very good secretarial job working for the government on Parliament Hill. She went all by herself and found a room in Ottawa. In those days, that was quite a brave thing for a young woman to do—and that's where she met my father.

Life on the farm in Ottawa was a lot of hard work for my father and his family, tending to the crops from early morning to night, taking them to market, buying seed and fertilizer, gauging the weather, praying for rain, and fixing the machinery. There wasn't a lot of time for a social life and meeting people. It was a tough life.

I had the impression that my father worked so many hours, he was never able to go out and meet any girls, and that's why he didn't tie the knot until he was in his forties. My father and mother met in town where he was selling produce from the farm. Even though she was about fourteen years younger than my dad, it didn't take long until they courted and decided to marry.

After their marriage, she continued working on Parliament Hill until she became pregnant with my older brother, Sheldon. (In those days women typically weren't allowed to keep working if they were going to have a baby.) Some time after Sheldon was born in 1946, the family moved to Cornwall.

I was born on October 12, 1948, and my little sister Sandra was born four years later, in 1952.

## My Maternal Grandparents

My mother's parents came from Eastern Europe and were born in Belarus. Sarah Cohen's father, Jacob Korubuchka (born in 1886), was from Turaŭ, and her mother, Peshe Golda Kaluznik (born in 1888), was born in Davyd-Haradok. They lived about forty kilometres apart in Southern Belarus. They sought refuge in Canada in the late 1800s because Eastern Europe was overrun with anti-Jewish pogroms. When they emigrated to North America, they changed their last name from Korubuchka to Cohen because it was easier to spell and sounded more North American. Two of my uncles later changed their names from Cohen to Caine in an effort to make it sound less Jewish. Since anti-semitism was quite evident in Canada at this time, they worried that prejudice would make it more difficult to find employment.

My mother shared stories about how her mother and older sister hid from the authorities in sheds in the country-side on their way across Russia to board a ship to Canada. Her father—my grandfather—left first, to find his family a safe place to live, and send them funds to join him. He had a sister already living in Winnipeg, and when he arrived, he sent money to my grandmother and aunt through the Red Cross. It took a long time for them to receive the money and travel across Russia, longer still to make the difficult sail to Canada, and then take the train over to Winnipeg. Amazingly, they managed to reunite and had seven more children in Winnipeg.

My mother's family of eight children, from eldest to youngest, includes:

Helen, born in 1914 (married Irvine Waldman);

Morris, born in 1921 (married Anne Snider);

Sarah, my mother, born in 1923 (married Oscar Niduvitch);

Harvey, born in 1924 (married Donna Weinberg);

Faye, born in 1926 (married Al Grant);

Bert, born in 1928 (married Helen Sweid);

Larry, born in 1930 (married Bernice Grushko);

Harry, born in 1931 (married Shirley Bakilinsky).

## My Paternal Grandparents

My father's father, Solomon Niduvitch (born in 1871), was
from Kyiv. My father's mother, Rachel Leah Niduvitch (born
in 1870), was from Odessa, so both of his parents were from
the Ukraine. Odessa is on the Black Sea, 476 kilometres from
Kyiv.

My paternal grandparents had nine children, and they
grew up on the family farm in Ottawa in an area called Eastview. My father was an easygoing person. He was like me,
a little withdrawn. Being one of the younger sons during
World War II, my father stayed in Ottawa to run the farm
while the rest of his brothers joined the army.

My dad's family consisted of six boys and three girls.
There was:

Mossie, born in 1890 (married Max Widder);

Jacob "Jake", born in 1895 (married Esther Pont);

Abe "Abie", born in 1896 (married Florence Reznik);

Alex "Alec", born in 1898 (married Marge Gallinger);

Michael "Mike", born in 1901(married Annie Schwartz-
berg);

Rebecca "Becky", born in 1903 (married Clem Gennis);

Oscar, my father, born in 1907 (married Sarah Cohen); Abraham "Irish", born in 1909 (married Bessie Lerner); Esther, born in 1911 (married Ben Hirsch).

Three of the brothers, Oscar, Alex, and Irish, all moved to Cornwall. Alex moved there first from the farm, then Irish, then my dad. Irish later moved to Florida and bought a motel across from the Hollywood Dog Track, a racetrack. He and his wife lived in Hallandale Beach. According to Fran, Irish's daughter, a census taker once came to their house in Eastview and asked his nationality and Abraham told them he was Irish. It then became the family joke and his permanent nickname.

There was an additional reason the nickname Irish was useful. Another brother was named Abe but called Abie, and he moved to Michigan. They were not given English names when they were born because they spoke Yiddish, so the family ended up with both an Abie and an Abraham. To avoid confusion, everyone always called Abraham "Irish."

Then there was Jake, who was much older than my father and lived in Montréal, then Michael, who moved to California. My dad's three sisters included Rebecca (also known as Aunt Becky), Mossie, and Esther, all of who stayed in Ottawa.

Before my grandparents (on my father's side) died, they bequeathed the family farm to my dad's eldest sister, Aunt Becky, to distribute when they passed. Unfortunately, she ignored their wishes and kept the income from the farm to herself. It was pretty well known within the family that most people didn't get along with Aunt Becky.

My parents left Ottawa for Cornwall to work with my Uncle Alex, who had a business doing maintenance and repairs on cars—and anything else he could fix. Alex was a very colourful fellow. He was always on the lookout for any opportunity. He pretty much did everything from soup to nuts. He owned a garage filled with tires, he sold motor parts—he'd sell anything that could be sold. He knew how early electronics worked and could fix all sorts of appliances. He would say yes to any broken-down appliance someone brought into his shop and then figure out how to repair it. Alex was a mechanical whiz.

When he was in his twenties, Alex was a smuggler during the Prohibition Era, when alcohol was outlawed in the United States. It was not legal in Canada from 1918 to 1920 as a wartime measure, but after World War I, Canada had free flowing booze that the US wanted. (America was under Prohibition from 1918 to 1933, causing organized crime to skyrocket.)

In both countries the Roaring Twenties also ushered in huge changes. For the first time, more people lived in cities than on farms, women called "flappers" cut their hair, shortened their skirts, listened to music on the radio (first broadcast in 1920), bought phonograph records, and danced in clubs during the Jazz Age. They also smoked, drank, and danced in speakeasies. To gain entry at the speakeasies, they had to recite a secret code, risking imprisonment from constant raids by police. Things were swinging during Prohibition and the ban on drinking made it all the more exciting. Alex complied by helping to quench the United States' growing thirst for alcohol.

There was one bridge across the St. Lawrence River between Montréal and Brockville, Ontario, and this was the only way to get across the river to America. Alex and his buddies had a car rigged up with train wheels on the front and back. Ten men would pick it up and place it on the railroad tracks, cram it full of booze, and drive it across the border. It would be unloaded on the other side in Massena, New York. Then the hooch would be driven down to a speakeasy in New York City owned by the famous gangster Al Capone.

One of my cousins told me a relative has a picture of my Uncle Alex with Al Capone. Later on, I found a newspaper article on the Internet about a time when Alex was taken into custody for smuggling alcohol inside the seat of his car.

Life was hard on farms in that era in Canada. The wheat market collapsed in the 1920s and the Depression took hold in the 1930s. It wasn't just the US that suffered after the stock market crash of 1929; Canada suffered horribly, and this drove people to do anything they could to feed their families and keep a roof over their heads. In my father's family alone, only one out of nine stayed on the farm—Aunt Becky. In 1919, not long after World War I ended, there was a popular song called "How Ya Gonna Keep 'Em Down on the Farm (After They've Seen Paree?)" The servicemen fighting in Europe had broadened their horizons and there was no going back. People weren't isolated anymore, especially with the advent of radio and TV, which became widespread after WWII. This would be the era that I was born into, now known as the baby boom generation.

# Chapter Two

## Family Life

Our childhood centred so much around extended family, almost every week we drove to Ottawa for visits. Before the seat belt days, Sheldon, Sandra, and I would just curl up on the backseat and fall asleep on the way home. My father's sister Esther, who wasn't married at the time, lived in the farmhouse with Becky and her husband, Clem. My father's eldest sister, Mossie, also lived in Ottawa. To us, she was more like a grandmother because she was so much older than my father. We'd get to visit them and see all sorts of cousins, but because my father was one of the youngest siblings, a lot of our cousins were much older than the three of us.

We called Aunt Esther "Esther the Kid Pester" because she loved to pinch our cheeks. She was probably such a rabid pincher because she didn't have children of her own and that was just her way of showing affection. She would never hug you—she would just walk up to you and before you knew it, she was pinching your cheeks. Sheldon got used to it, but my little sister and I just hated it. We didn't want to go near her because we didn't want to be pinched.

In Cornwall, my father worked in his body shop, called Deluxe Garage, and he and my mother and my brother, Sheldon, lived above the garage, down a back lane, behind a row of tenements. This is where I was born, in October of 1948. My sister Sandra was born in the same year that my Uncle Alex died.

Uncle Alex was in the garage when he had a heart attack. Clutching his chest through the pain, he was able to tell my father that if he died, my dad should go find the money he had hidden in the walls of his house. Alex was taken to the hospital in Cornwall and transferred over to Royal Victoria Hospital in Montréal, where he lingered for about a week.

My father went to Montréal to see him and was with him at the end, as were Aunt Becky and Aunt Esther, who came from Ottawa to say good-bye. Uncle Alex died on February 22, 1952. Alex's wife, Marge, had died two years before and they had no children, so Alex left everything to my dad.

After the shock of Alex's sudden death, his burial, and a spate of grieving for his brother, my father told us he essentially smashed up the walls of Alex's place looking for his socked-away life savings. When he found the stash of cash, he discovered that he had bequeathed him enough money to build a new house in a better neighbourhood.

Uncle Alex's death also spurred my father on to start buying and selling cars, and he started a driving school for additional income.

We weren't rich, but we weren't poor either. When my dad built our new house on Fourth Avenue, he had enough money to pay for one other worker. He hired a friend of his from Ottawa, and this man lived with us for about seven or eight months. They had a little help at times from other tradesmen, but the house was basically built by the two of them. My dad's friend was a nice old guy, older than my father, a Polish man who had a little trouble with English but was really pleasant and a super-talented carpenter. He knew where to get the right supplies, and he finished his tasks quickly.

They built a fairly different house, designed by my mother's brother Bert. The house was out of character with the neighbourhood, which was an old southern Ontario neighbourhood with the typical bungalows with peaked roofs. The new home was a two-storey, concrete-block, apartment-style triplex. Our family lived on the bottom floor. We rented out two apartments on the top floor so we had some steady income to rely on.

In the new house on Fourth Avenue, our kitchen was quite basic, but it was my mother's favourite place. We had a fifties-style kitchen table with a band of chrome around it. The living room sported an L-shaped couch, rounded at the end, which was always covered in plastic; my mother always covered her furniture in plastic so it wouldn't get damaged. There wasn't much artwork or decoration on the walls. The interior was rather plain as decorating wasn't really important to my mother.

While I was growing up, my mother was very attentive. She would always be up early making us breakfast. My father was selling cars by then and had sold a car for one thousand dollars to a dairy farm in exchange for milk, cheese, and eggs, so that's what we had for breakfast every morning. When we didn't clean our plates, my mother was famous for saying,

"Eat! Eat! People in Europe are starving." I guess that's what she was used to hearing during the war.

With all the dairy products we had in the house, I came to love curds. When milk is left overnight in a warm place, it coagulates and thickens, then the watery whey is drained off and the curds (or cottage cheese) are the result. All my life I've loved cottage cheese and would eat it all the time.

My mother would always tuck us into bed and tell us stories at night. She would read to us before we went to sleep—classics like *The Adventures of Tom Sawyer* and *Huckleberry Finn*, which we liked a lot. She was a caring person. And she was also a devoted knitter. She would always be knitting us mittens or new sweaters. Basically she couldn't sit still. She was a busy woman. Later in life, when I had my own children, she was very involved in their lives as well.

My father operated his businesses and my mother was the business administrator. She kept the books. She made all the appointments for his driving school, did the billing, and paid all of their bills. Basically she ran the office. Her memory was absolutely phenomenal, and the way she would chat with anyone, she would know their entire life history in ten minutes. She was such an affable, good-natured person, genuinely interested in other people.

My father was a steady, hard worker who was out every day in whatever business he was doing at the time. My mom was affectionate and warm, and food was a big part of our life—that was how my mother showed her love for us kids. My mother loved baking and cooking. We were a meat and potatoes family: there was a roast and potatoes almost every night.

She was a great baker. Her cakes and pastries were delicious. She made an incredible poppy seed cake with a special technique that made it especially light, fluffy, and spongy. My aunt, who made me one of those cakes, says she used extra-large eggs—that's the secret. My mother also made something called kuffels. This was dough rolled up in cinnamon with coconut inside. It was basically a cinnamon bun rolled sideways instead of round-ways.

My parents got along pretty well. My mother knew what she wanted and my father wasn't the kind of guy to argue. It was difficult to get him upset or riled up. I think it was fun for him to have a lively woman in his life after being single for so long. My mom would come up with ideas and he would follow through on them. He was a good dad and spent time teaching us his many useful skills.

Sheldon used to follow him around as my dad was doing business, visiting different suppliers, and he would sit and listen to their conversations, while I would stay home and read. I was more studious and Sheldon was more outgoing and relaxed, getting up and putting on whatever clothes he could grab to go out early with my father. As for me, I always wanted to look sharp, making sure my clothes were clean, pressed, and that they fit well.

A fond memory I have of Cornwall was when I was really young. In the wintertime, the milkman would deliver whole milk and the cream would freeze on the top and push up the little cardboard stopper. We not only had a milkman, but he delivered milk by horse and buggy before they changed over to trucks.

Another fond memory was the little dog we had, who was fun to play with. She would actually walk us to school and find her way back home alone. Then she would meet us at school to walk us home for lunch. Rinnie was a fox terrier and she was the best dog a kid could have.

We were lucky that we had a great place to play in the wintertime and that our father liked to spend time with us outside. We had a small sliding hill nearby that Sandra, Sheldon, and I would toboggan down when there was snow.

In the fall, before the snow, my father would put up boards and build a hockey and skating rink in our backyard. He was very keen on that. The rink was around twelve feet by twenty feet, and we'd help him gather and lay down fallen leaves to protect the grass. Then he would go out and water the rink with the hose. If it snowed, we would help tamp down the snow and he'd water it again.

The ice was never very smooth. It's harder than it looks to make really smooth ice. Still, we were able to play hockey and Sandra and I would play games on the ice. I had weak ankles but it was still fun. The kids in the neighbourhood would come and play on our rink. Sheldon was a better skater than I was; he even played hockey with some of the junior hockey leagues. He was the bigger of the two of us at all of five feet, four inches!

My father played a lot of hockey when he was younger; that's probably why he was so eager to build us a rink. Our neighbours even showed us a trophy his team won, with his name on it. They had a relative who was on his team.

Sometimes we would skate on the Ottawa Canal. It was built about one hundred years ago to connect the St. Lawrence River to the Ottawa River. You could see hundreds of people skating up and down the river under an archway of snow-laden branches. It was so beautiful and was such a classic image it could have been in the 1800s.

In the summertime we had a garden and my dad was always showing us the vegetables and herbs and how to care for them. I guess you couldn't take the farmer out of him. I learned a lot of skills from my dad, including how to use tools, because he was always doing something in the garage behind the house. Like a lot of farmers, my father couldn't just call a tradesman any time he needed something done, so he learned carpentry, welding, and plumbing, and how to fix the farm machinery.

At home, my dad had a huge air compressor and all kinds of pneumatic tools, so we were able to make a tree house in the field out back. We hammered steps into the tree so Sheldon and Sandra and I could climb up there. One of the neighbours complained that we were banging nails into the poor, innocent tree, but the tree survived. Our little tree house looked dangerous, but it was actually pretty sturdy. The cardboard we covered it with didn't last very long, just until the rains came. Still, it was great to have our own special little place for a while.

## Fifty-two First Cousins

Our holidays weren't big resort type holidays, no Disneyland or anything like that. Many summers we visited my mother's family in Winnipeg. Again, it was all about family. We would drive up to Winnipeg to visit my maternal grandparents. We'd stay with my Aunt Faye and play with her kids. One special year, on the way, we saw Babe the Big Blue Ox. We got out of the car and had our pictures taken with the huge statue of Paul Bunyan and this unbelievably blue creature.

We went south through Minnesota and by Lake Michigan to reach Winnipeg. When we stopped the car for gas, the mosquitoes would get in and be all over us in an instant. I remember the first time we travelled on a big ferry across Lake Michigan. I'd never been on a ferry where you drive your whole car onto it, and that was exciting.

In Winnipeg, my mother's parents had been farmers too, but by the time we met them, they had leased out their farm. Still, they had a big chicken coop in the backyard even though they lived in the middle of town.

Coming from White Russia near Minsk, what is called Belarus today, my mother's parents didn't speak English very well. My grandfather could be understood better, since he needed to learn English to conduct business. But my grandmother took care of the house and the farm animals, so she didn't have much interaction with the outside world.

By the time my grandmother had cleaned up breakfast it was time to start lunch. She spent her life in that kitchen, pulling feathers off chickens and washing and cutting up the vegetables from the garden, doing all these things that most people don't do anymore, that a butcher or grocer would take care of. My grandparents were still used to doing things the old way, so we enjoyed fresh poultry, eggs, and vegetables from the garden.

As I mentioned, my father came from a family of nine, and my mother came from a family of eight. My brother and sister and I had a total of fifty-two first cousins between the two families! Many of my mom's brothers and sisters still lived in this same area where they grew up, and those eight kids each had lots of kids our age. The cousins we had in Ottawa were much older, but the kids in Winnipeg were the perfect age for us to play with. It was a wonderful experience going back there and interacting with so many cousins.

Playing baseball outside my aunt's house, Sheldon accidentally threw the ball through her large plate glass window. We'd talk about that all the time when we were reminiscing, how someone missed the catch and broke that window.

We went back a few times and took an excursion to a large gravel pit. The farm was in Birds Hill, about thirty miles out of town. There was a quarry there, and when it was no longer in use, it filled with water and people started using it as a beach. It's now a provincial park with sand around the water. In Winnipeg we would also go to the zoo. They had a fantastic zoo there. But most of the time was spent hanging around, relaxing and visiting family.

My earliest memory of a vacation staying in a resort area, rather than visiting relatives, was when I was about four years old. We took a summer trip to Old Orchard Beach, in Maine. We went with the family down the street who had two kids about our age. Back then Orchard Beach was known as "The Coney Island of Maine." We rode the roller coasters, ate ice cream and cotton candy, and had a blast driving the bumper cars and smashing into each other. We stayed in these little cabins and took walks on the beach, picking up sea glass and stones and shells.

The first time my siblings and I had ever encountered pizza was in Maine. We couldn't figure out what it was—it smelled so horrible because of the melted cheese. We just could not imagine how people could eat that stuff.

Other than those vacations, our family mainly took short trips. We went to North Pole, New York, the site of Santa's Workshop, near Syracuse, about three hours away, and to Meacham Lake, also in New York, which was a little more than an hour from Cornwall. It was always great to swim in any lake and play on a beach.

Our winter vacations were also spent visiting family, and this was extra special because we could visit Uncle Irish at his motel in Florida. We actually visited for longer that just the week of winter break. Our parents believed we got more education travelling through the states by car than staying in school in Cornwall in December, so we would take two to three weeks and go down to Florida, where it was blissfully warm. On the way, we would stop in Pennsylvania and then Georgia to stay overnight, so it would take three to four days for us to get there.

We spent a lot of time having fun at the motel, swimming in the pool, going to the beach, and touring around the area. The motel was a third-rate motel—the kind I wouldn't stay at today, but back then we didn't care.

My Uncle Irish was a lot like my father—rather quiet—but his wife, Bessie, was an outgoing woman. She knew all the neighbours and was very social like my mom, always meeting friends for lunch or for coffee, and she talked a mile a minute. She was involved in everything. He did the physical work around the motel and she took care of the administration, collecting money from the guests and handling the problems that came up. I think they enjoyed having family there and some kids to brighten up the place, and we sure were happy to ditch school and travel someplace warm.

## Chapter Three

# Scouting, Hobbies, and Budding Entrepreneurship

I joined the Cub Scouts when I was little and was very much involved in the Scouting movement, keen on earning all the badges I could. Many of them had to do with being outdoors, which I loved. Orienteering was one of them, zeroing in on a destination on a map and being able to get there guided by a compass. There was also signalling with flags, which ships at sea had to do when they were in distress. I also received a badge for learning Morse code. I suppose I was ready for any emergency!

I started at Cubs, and then went to Scouts, all the way up to the highest level, the Rover Scouts. I loved Scouting and the outdoors so much when I was young that I became a Cub leader and then a Scout leader with my own kids. I'm still friends with other leaders that I worked with twenty years ago.

My dad would attend the ceremonies where we got our badges, and both Mom and Dad would help us put together mattress pads and rolls of canvas that the Scouts used for exercising to guard us against the hard floor. Sheldon was active in the Scouts as well.

One proud moment for me at school was when I received the Best-Dressed Cadet Award from the Glengarry Highlanders. This group of soldiers defended the north bank of the St. Lawrence River in the Revolutionary War, and in all the wars since—the War of 1812, and WW I and II. They were known for their bravery and high standards, and they guarded the canals around Cornwall, fought on D-day in France and all through Europe in World War II.

They gave out certificates for the best marcher, best dressed, and so on. My brother even won for being able to take a gun apart and put it back together the fastest. (Some boys could do this blindfolded!) At school, once a week instead of PE, we'd do military exercises, marching around the field, switching rifles from right to left, holding the guns up and down—what you'd see at a parade ground.

On the playground the day I received my award, I was wearing a MacIntosh Clan tartan. I polished my spats and ironed my kilt carefully, and I looked pretty spiffy. The girls had blue skirts and the boys had kilts. It was a big honour to be acknowledged by the Highlanders, so it was a proud moment for me.

When I was in Cub Scouts, we'd go camping and play around the Swansea Rapids, but when I was ten they were blocked off and all the houses were relocated. These neighbouring areas around Cornwall became known as The Lost Villages when they were permanently flooded in 1958. Construction of the St. Lawrence Seaway and the subsequent power dam required a brand new, larger reservoir, and this is where they put it. The rapids dried up when they diverted the water upstream.

Underneath the rapids were all these huge rocks that had fallen in. We would crawl around looking for Indian arrowheads and artifacts from the War of 1812, where land and naval battles were fought along the St. Lawrence River. It was fun to search for them and we'd let out a whoop when we found a treasure, then take it home to display on our dressers.

Sometimes there were large distances between the rocks, and one time I jumped from too great a height down into the riverbed and split a bone in my leg. I ended up with a bone infection called osteomyelitis, which people used to die from. Luckily there was an antibiotic by that time that could treat it—although I did spend quite a bit of time in the hospital.

It was just awful to be lying in that hospital, bedridden for the entire summer and part of the fall. Every day I endured painful antibiotic injections into my injured leg. I absolutely could not move because my leg hurt so much, and I needed assistance to get to the washroom and back. After a couple months I could walk a bit on my own in my hospital room.

The big fear with this condition was the possibility of amputation. My family found out later on that many people had lost limbs from this infection, so I was glad I knew nothing about that or I would have had plenty of time to worry lying in that hospital bed. Finally I was released and gradually got strong enough to play ball again.

I was always in the hardball or softball league at home. I also played broomball in the street in front of our house, like street hockey. I was shy and didn't do a lot of group things. I never took up curling like a lot of people I knew. I wish I had done more things like that because people get a lot out of group events, but I did do some skating at an open skate on Friday and Saturday nights. I was never a great skater, but I did all right and had some fun with it.

It didn't help that I grew up to be only a little over five feet, one inch—a bit on the short side. I was always the last one in class picked for the baseball and hockey teams. That certainly affected me. At times, I felt like an outsider. I wanted to be part of the group, but I could never quite get into the "in crowd."

I was slightly withdrawn for the early part of my life, all the way through high school, until a few years after university, then I started coming out of my shell. One thing that helped was learning how things worked, how to fix them, and the entrepreneurial exploits I did on my own.

Of course, I have my father and my uncle to thank for teaching me so many things. My dad certainly learned a lot from his brother, and I learned so much from my dad. Even though Uncle Alex was a bit of a character, he really had helped my dad and our family in so many ways. He gave us a new home and gave my dad a new life away from the farm.

As I mentioned, after Uncle Alex died, my father became more entrepreneurial. He branched out a little in the automotive world. He became a driving instructor and he also travelled to Montréal to buy cars at auction and bring them to Cornwall to sell. That was his main job for many years. He would have about six or seven of his cars at any one dealer. I remember one time a dealer passed away and he took over his car lot. The money from that allowed him to build a bigger body shop.

There wasn't enough room at the car lot for all of the cars, so he had to bring some home to work on them. There was only a little hut at the car lot with some basic tools, no real cover from the cold and the elements, but at home he could use the garage.

Mechanical devices were much more transparent in those days. When I was older, someone gave me an old car from 1956 and I was able to change the engine on it. I couldn't do that today. Engines are much more complicated and it takes computers to diagnose what's going on with them.

I really do believe I got my entrepreneurial spirit from my father. Things were changing quite a bit in that era and people had to adapt—it was a time of some really big changes. TV was in almost every household and cars got more sophisticated.

Seeing the resourcefulness of my father influenced me quite a bit. I used to watch my dad repair cars and appliances. My father taught me how to solder wires in radios and clocks and other electronics; he taught me how to change tires, fix flats, and clean spark plugs. As a kid, I felt he knew everything. He could look at something and figure out how to fix it. He had a mechanic's brain. He would teach me about carpentry as well.

Later in my life, I also liked to repair all sorts of things, from electronics to broken furniture. I ended up doing a lot of carpentry, too, and I built my own furniture. I made all of our children's bunk beds, crafted a dining room hutch and my family's kitchen table. I actually tried to make chairs once, but they weren't successful. I did make a glass étagère that turned out pretty well. I have every kind of tool there is, a table saw, a band saw, a planer. If there's a tool out there, I have it. My dad would have been so impressed! I'm sure he would have loved to experiment with all of these state-of-the-art tools.

I've really enjoyed woodworking and get such a sense of satisfaction seeing a finished product that I've made with my own two hands. In my profession of pharmacy, there is no finished product—you aren't producing anything. In woodworking you end up with something solid and finite; you can see it, touch it, use it.

I tried to emulate my dad and my uncle as a kid by finding ways to make money. I was always involved in contests through my school. I wanted to sell the most Halloween candy so badly, so that I could win a bike, but someone else outsold me. Then the YMCA had a contest for selling tickets to the sports fair, and I sold the most tickets and won the bicycle.

Sheldon had a *Star Weekly* paper route and I told him I wanted to sell *Star Weekly*s too, so Sheldon said, "Well, go out and get your own customers." So I went door to door and got my own customers. I could be very enterprising and I was not afraid to talk to people. I had finally found something I was really good at, and I made fifty cents a paper per week with my paper route.

This gave me a glimpse into how to become successful later in life. My thought process naturally would come up with new ways of doing things, and I was willing to take risks when I needed to take them.

# Chapter Four
## Tragedy Strikes

On November 20, 1957, when I was at school in fourth grade, I was notified that I needed to rush home immediately because of a family emergency. I felt a little scared on my way home, not knowing what awaited me. When I opened the front door, everyone was in a panic; there were police, insurance people, neighbours, and all sorts of strangers in the house. My parents drew me away from the commotion, sat me down, and told me that my little sister, Sandra, had been hit by a car and died. She was five years old and was walking to the park with a babysitter when a car came zooming by and did not stop.

I was so mad, I ran to my room and picked up the first thing I could find—an ice skate—and said, "I'm going to kill that guy." I wanted revenge. There was so much anxiety swirling inside me; I didn't know what to do with it. So much anguish in our house!

At night, talk would loom up and then quiet down about court cases and lawsuits against the driver, and I would hear snippets, mostly my parents discussing it in whispers when I was in bed. I wished I could have done something about it, but what could I do?

My mom did not take it well at all. She was crying all the time, in despair really. Of course, when it happened I cried—everyone was crying—but my mother's sobbing went on for weeks. I felt helpless and remained at a loss for what to do. I wished I could have made things better, but I had no power to change anything. One by one, pictures drawn by Sandra that were on the refrigerator and photographs of her disappeared from display. I was too young to understand how horrible this was for my mother.

My dad carried on with his same routine. He was working long hours, getting up early and arriving home late some nights, so we didn't interact very much. Nobody really talked about Sandra after a while. We went to our own corners and dealt with it individually as best we could.

My mom and dad didn't allow Sheldon and me to go to the funeral. I think they made the right decision. It was a traumatic time all through the trial, as the driver was brought up on charges and my mother had to keep reliving the pain. Finally, it was ruled an accident and my parents received a bit of money from the settlement, but the emotional scars lasted for years.

Sandra died so very early, at five years old. We kids all played together and got along with her so well. When you look at our old photo albums you can see pictures of us playing in the yard. Her death left a void that could never be filled.

## A New Baby Sister

About nine months later, my mother gave birth to another girl, and she was named Bonnie. She was born in 1958, ten years younger than me. In those days, doctors encouraged women to have another child as a way to get over the loss. It was probably a good thing for my mother to have a new baby to get her mind off the grief of losing Sandra, and she showered her love on my little sister.

When you look at pictures of Sandra and Bonnie, they looked so much alike. Even when Bonnie looks at the old pictures, she has to check the dates to tell if it's Sandra or herself.

Sheldon and I had a saying back then: "What Bonnie wants, Bonnie gets." Yes, she was spoiled, but we understood how that could happen. My mom was so glad to have her; Bonnie brought her joy back.

Bonnie is a lot like our mom. She's very outgoing, loves to entertain and get everyone together. Bonnie married Mel Bauer in 1987 and they have two boys, Michael and Brian. Their house is always open to family dropping by, just like my mother's. They often host family dinners and lunches for the Jewish holidays. She is such a good cook and everyone always has a good time at Bonnie's place!

## Chapter Five

# Growing up Jewish

When I grew up, Cornwall was a small town of forty-three thousand, and its population is only slightly larger today. Back in the 1950s there were not many Jewish families and only about five Jewish kids in my whole school. We were a real minority. There was always some anti-Semitism, but it was under the surface, such as Jewish children not being invited to parties.

A boy in my class asked me to play at his house a few times until his grandmother told me I could not come over anymore because I killed Christ. Things like that would happen. People would say things that didn't make much sense to two kids who just wanted to play together.

When I turned thirteen, my parents made sure to make my Bar Mitzvah special. Relatives all the way from Ottawa and Montréal came to see my on my special day. Even my grandparents travelled all the way from Winnipeg. My father had a custom suit made for me. It was handy that my father knew the man who owned the suit factory. It was hard to find a suit for someone my size. I would wear the same suit again for my high school graduation!

My friend Stanley was the boy who lived next door. We both had Bar Mitzvahs around the same time and we stayed good friends for years, even when Stanley moved away to Montréal and then to Toronto after the Quebec separatist movement. It was fun to share the highs and lows with a friend—one of the lows being learning Hebrew.

After school, twice a week, my brother and I would take Hebrew classes at the synagogue. There was a dairy in the middle of town that used horses to pull milk carts. It was just out the back door of the synagogue, so the school would allow us to drink chocolate milk. That was how they got us to go to the classes, because everyone wanted this tasty treat. It was absolutely scrumptious. It was thick and chocolaty and creamy and made with whole milk, which you don't see much of anymore. I don't think it made me learn my Hebrew any better, but it sure was delicious. I remember the milk more than the Hebrew!

Sheldon and I both had problems with Hebrew. I'm sure lots of kids think there's something wrong with them if they struggle with it, but it's not uncommon to have problems with this language. The reason was that no one really spoke Hebrew around us so there were few people to practise with. I think the rabbi who taught us just didn't know how to encourage us to learn another language.

Another issue was that our grandparents spoke Yiddish, not Hebrew. The Ashkenazi Jews from Germany spoke Yiddish, which is an outgrowth of the Old High German language. When these Jews spread to Eastern Europe, they brought that language with them. Yiddish became the language of trade, so Jews from Russia could speak with Jews from Germany and Poland. And when they emigrated to North America, they might have had trouble with English, but they could speak Yiddish to many new immigrants from different countries.

By contrast, Hebrew was the biblical language, which was almost dead until 1945, when it was decided that it should be the language of the new country of Israel. There wasn't anybody speaking it. The Jews in North Africa and Spain spoke a language called Ladino, which was similar to what Yiddish was in those countries. Sheldon's son's mother-in-law is from Greece and she speaks Ladino, a mixture of Hebrew and Spanish. Sheldon knows enough Spanish that they can have a conversation.

So many colourful and "sounds like what it is" descriptive and evocative Yiddish words have moved into the English language, with Jewish comedians and entertainers being broadcast all over the world on radio and TV.

So that's another reason there weren't many people to help us with Hebrew, certainly not our parents. Another factor in my struggle with it was that I missed a lot of the basic foundational work in many subjects, including Hebrew, when I was in the hospital with osteomyelitis.

But I got through my Bar Mitzvah without any trouble and received lots of love, well wishes, and presents from friends and relatives. I remember getting a football, several pens, a gold Krugerrand (a South African coin), some money, and a baseball glove.

I had a big party afterward, and everyone my parents knew in the whole town was invited. I'm sure it was in the hundreds. All the girls were taller than I was. That was the age when girls grew more quickly than boys, but I was short anyway. It was fun dancing and seeing everyone having a good time, especially my friends and my parents.

I remember watching my Bar Mitzvah movies with my mother years later. She would point out someone and say, "Oh, that's Mr. and Mrs. So-and-So, they're dead," and "There's Mrs. So-and-So, she's dead." I think they were all dead!

My children were more involved in Jewish activities than we were. Cornwall only had sixty Jewish families and one little synagogue. Ottawa in those days had three synagogues. And compared to the social life of my kids, in my youth Cornwall would have one Bar Mitzvah every three or four years. When my children were coming of age in Vancouver, there was a Bar Mitzvah or Bat Mitzvah almost every week.

Judaism has always been an important part of my family's life; it makes us feel like we are part of a community. I have never been super religious, but the culture, customs, common history, and connection to Israel are important to me.

## Summer Camp

A place where I felt most comfortable being Jewish was at summer camp. When I was a kid, my brother and I went away to summer camp for eight weeks to a place called Camp Maccabee, and that's where I got my love of nature. Even my sister Bonnie went there for a month when she was only six years old. The owner of the camp was once the mayor of Côte-Saint-Luc, a suburb of Montréal.

There were seven or eight cabins each for the boys and the girls, fronting a lovely lake called Trout Lake. It was an old hotel with cabins before they split it up so the boys would be separate from the girls. I started going to camp when I was nine or ten and went every year until I was a counsellor at the camp. Then I went to another camp near Ottawa as a counsellor too.

Cornwall was very hot and muggy during the summers (it isn't known as the armpit of Canada for nothing), and while it was great to be away in the piney mountains where it was cooler, at times I would still become homesick. We'd play games like kick the can and red rover. Ours was a particularly small camp though, so when other camps would visit and we'd play baseball, we would always lose. Those camps were much larger and might have two or three hundred kids. There was a whole group of Jewish camps that would play each other.

We did have rowboats and canoes, and I discovered that I loved canoeing. There were only six canoes, so we had to do a lot of sharing! We were able to glide out on the water a couple times a week on the canoes, race and splash around, and paddle back to enjoy campfires and s'mores on special nights.

One week they divided up the camp between the blue and white teams and we put on a show with skits and songs. It was a competition, but I didn't go up on stage. I couldn't entertain. When I was in school I did try out a few things to see if I had any talent. I took tap dancing and played in the rhythm band at school. My instrument was the clarinet, but I wasn't very good at it. I enjoyed it, but I found it difficult to stay on key. It's something you're born with—and I wasn't. But watching the other kids perform was great.

At camp, we were also given a one- to two-hour break each day where we were supposed to nap or write letters home. Many years later, I was rummaging through some keepsakes and saw an old postcard my brother wrote home from camp that read, "Please send me a pocketknife." I could not imagine my parents sending a potential weapon through the mail to him, and I'm quite sure they never did.

After four weeks, there would be an open house where families could visit. Some kids stayed for four weeks and they'd be going home, but for us eight-weekers, we were able to see our parents for a day or two before we were on our own again. My father and mother stayed at a place nearby. It was a six-hour drive from Cornwall, so they couldn't do a day trip. It was always great for me to spend time with my parents and they enjoyed getting away from the city.

We sent all of our kids to a Jewish summer camp as well. The camp was down by Olympia, Washington, and they would travel there by bus. They were gone for three weeks. My son, Kevin, met a girl, Robin Zemble from Portland, in his Jewish youth group, and they became counsellors there and at another Jewish camp where they spent the summers. They eventually got married and now they have a little boy.

# Chapter Six
## Life Changes in an Instant

My parents were fairly easygoing with us. Since Sheldon was the oldest, I'd look to him to see what we could or could not do, as we became teenagers. For example, when Sheldon started driving, he didn't have a curfew—but his car did. He'd have to be back home before midnight and hang up the keys. Then he'd go out again without the car. My mom and dad knew we were out late at night, but as long as we weren't driving, they were okay with that.

Sheldon graduated high school and went to college in Ottawa, and one weekend four of his friends drove to Cornwall for a visit. It was getting late and Sheldon asked if they could stay over. Mom said that was fine and she just made up some beds in the basement. It was nothing for her to have Sheldon and four friends stay. The house was always open for parties, with people coming and going or just hanging out. My mom was a social person, so she understood how teens wanted to be with their friends.

When Sheldon went to college, Aunt Becky entered the picture. We kids were aware of all the bad blood from all the stories we heard about her. She was the matriarch of the family and she controlled everything. So when Sheldon decided he wanted to go to school in Ottawa, my parents figured that it would be nice for Aunt Becky to have his company, someone to take care of her, as she was getting older.

So Sheldon spent his first two years of technical school in Ottawa living with Aunt Becky. Here he was a teenager off to university and he's living with this old lady and her outmoded values. Not only that, she gave him a curfew. My parents gave us so much freedom in high school and now he had this elderly aunt telling him what to do. I was almost finished with high school and thinking about what I'd like to do with my life. After watching what Sheldon went through, going to school in Ottawa was not on my list. Instead, I decided to go to University of Western Ontario, near London.

On typical Sunday mornings, the whole family would sleep in and watch TV and generally be lazy. One winter weekend, my sister, Bonnie, was watching cartoons with my father in the bedroom when she came running into the living room, saying, "Daddy's breathing funny! Daddy's not breathing right!"

My mother and I rushed into the other room and found my dad with drool coming out of his mouth, struggling for breath. My mom tried to perform CPR on him until the ambulance came.

There was a doctor who lived down the street, so I ran to his house. He said he was having breakfast and he'd be there in a few minutes, but by the time he got there the ambulance had already arrived.

My father passed away right then and there. My mother was crying, and the rest of us were twisted up into a panic. The emergency workers told us the clot in his heart was too big. We watched helplessly as they took him to the ambulance. I never saw him again. I was in a daze at how quickly it all happened.

Sheldon came down from Ottawa and wanted to see my father one more time, so they opened the casket for him, but normally in the Jewish religion they don't have open caskets.

It was such a shock for everyone. My dad was sixty-one when he died. My mother was much younger than he was—by fourteen years. I'm sure in the back of her mind she knew he would die first, but she probably never thought he would go that early in life, and that fast. My dad died in my last year of high school, in February of 1967, when I was in grade thirteen.

While my little sister and I tried to cope with the loss, my mother didn't show any outward signs of distress or money worries; she kept it together pretty well. She did what needed to be done, and she shielded us from the details, especially the economic impact. We really had no idea how dire our circumstances were with no breadwinner.

After my father's death, everything shifted. It was one of those things that just happens—and then your whole life changes. There we were, the four of us, with no assets in place. My mother had not worked since the war when she typed up the manifest for cargo ships, so it wasn't as if she was bringing in a steady income. We had the house and another piece of land that wasn't worth very much. My father's driving school consisted of him and no one else, so when he was gone, there went the school—there wasn't any money to get out of that.

The house was paid for, so that was good, and we could have received a little bit of rent from the upstairs apartments, but my mom still wouldn't have been able to afford putting my brother and me through university. Bonnie, was only eight years old. We had to do something or we would be destitute.

When my mother's brother, Uncle Harry, drove out for the funeral from Vancouver, he told our family there was no point in staying in Cornwall since there was nobody left. Some family on my father's side still lived in Ottawa, but we were not close with them, and we had no other relatives in Cornwall.

We couldn't see how we could swing two college educations without any income, so Uncle Harry asked our family to move to Vancouver. He was a pharmacist and had a store in Vancouver on Oak Street. My mother saw that we had no options, and just said,

"I guess we're going to Vancouver." The move to Vancouver was very smart in retrospect. It gave us so many opportunities we would never have had in Cornwall.

My mother sold off a lot of our belongings. Back then it cost an enormous amount to ship things or put them on a truck and haul them long distances, especially anything heavy, since it was measured by weight.

It felt surreal to me, as if I were being launched out of a rocket. Here my dad was just gone without as much as a good-bye. And it was decided that I was going to the University of British Columbia and I wasn't even accepted yet. It felt traumatic not knowing what was around the corner. I would be thrust into a whole new world, with all these people I did not know.

At the time, Sheldon was going to EOIT (Eastern Ontario Institute of Technology) studying social work. He was lucky to get into BCIT (British Columbia Institute of Technology), and I was fortunate that I did indeed get into UBC. What was unfortunate, however, was that the government cut off so much funding for social services after Sheldon graduated that he ended up moving to the Northwest Territory, where things were cheaper. We went to visit him with the whole family a few times, but the reality was that I saw my brother much less, and the only close family I'd have around me at this time were my mother and my sister.

## Vancouver, Here We Come

When we moved to Vancouver we found a rental to start with. It was cold and drafty, built on a slab, so the floor was always frigid in the fall and winter. The cold drifted up and lingered in your bones. That was in Marpole near Seventieth Avenue, and after about a year we moved over to Nineteenth Avenue. We were there a couple years; then, in 1970, my mother bought a duplex on Cambie Street with money left over from selling the house in Cornwall, a very smart investment for her. She stayed there for many years, until we had to move her into an apartment because she couldn't go up and down the stairs.

My mom found a job at the Beth Israel synagogue as a bookkeeper. If you wanted to know who was married to whom, where they lived, or what they did for a living, my mother knew it all. She knew everybody in town and everybody knew my mother.

The reason she was so well known in the community was because anyone who paid their bills to the synagogue had to go through her, and she was naturally so friendly and outgoing. She played mah-jongg quite a bit; she had four or five different mah-jongg groups, so she played almost every day.

As I started attending UBC, at least I didn't have to stay in the residences. I could drive from our new home, so that saved money. We also had the support from some of the family in the city.

I had always liked my Uncle Harry and tried to emulate him, so I suppose that's how I ended up in pharmacy. I worked in his store quite a bit, every Saturday and Sunday and nights while I was going to school.

When I first went to UBC, I was so unprepared. I felt lost in Vancouver. Compared to Cornwall, Vancouver was totally different. It was so much bigger. The university alone had twenty thousand people (about half the entire city of Cornwall) and the city had about a million. I pretty much didn't know anybody, and I was thrust into this huge metropolis. I was in the Faculty of Science and the courses were so hard. Basic principles had been left out of my education, so I had a lot of catching up to do.

Back in Cornwall, I had completed grade thirteen. (This was when Ontario still had grade thirteen and three years of university instead of four.) At the university, they allowed me into the second year in certain courses. Realizing too late that grade thirteen was not equivalent to the first year of university I had an especially tough time keeping up. Taking first year would have been hard enough, but being thrown into second year courses was just overwhelming. That year was basically a write-off.

I tried to get help from some of the professors and they just assumed I should already know the curriculum. I should never have gone into second-year chemistry with the education I had in Cornwall, but I did. So there I was, trying to take courses without the proper foundation. Somehow I managed to squeeze through and I didn't fail any courses that year.

The next year I found microbiology to be a lot easier. I didn't have to do all the mathematics calculations and other complicated figuring. I took some genetics courses and other science courses as well. But Chemistry 203 and Chemistry 205 are two of the hardest courses, and I didn't have the fundamentals of having completed Chemistry 120 to help me.

I was pretty much alone. I would go to the campus and wander from class to class, seeing thousands of people but not knowing any of them. I didn't have time to get to know anyone because I was constantly trying to keep up with my classes.

I did have an opportunity to join a fraternity and my uncle thought it would be a good idea for me to join, but I was too shy and didn't have the self-confidence. That may have been a mistake, because if I had joined at least I would have had people to talk to and get some advice on my courses.

I managed to make it through the first year and worked hard until I earned a Bachelor of Science degree in 1970.

The problem was, I didn't know what the degree was good for. It wasn't a bachelor's degree in anything specific. I had chemistry, physics, biology, and microbiology, but this listing of credits didn't point me in any clear direction. So I decided to go into pharmacy, which meant I would have to go back to school for another four years.

## Chapter Seven

# European Vacation

One of the highlights of my university years was the summer I travelled to Europe with four other guys. I travelled through Europe in a Comer van with my cousin Ken Waldman and three friends, Allan Nutkiewicz, Ken Garfinkel, and Peter Kafka. We were sitting around one day and just decided to go to Europe. Everyone was going to Europe back then.

We purchased the van in London through a buy-and-re-sell plan with the British Columbia Automobile Association before we left. When we were done in August they would buy the van back for a fixed amount. It was a good deal because a lot of kids were bumming around Europe, and come September, everyone was trying to sell their vehicles at the same time.

We visited many countries. Allan was really good at organizing and he had the map all drawn out. We started in England and went across to France, then into Spain and Portugal, and along through Monaco and down the coast to Italy. We went back up the other side of Italy to Switzerland, then back down through Yugoslavia and across the border into Macedonia. We left the van in Greece for a week and flew to Israel.

After that we went back up north and toured Bulgaria, Austria, Germany, Luxembourg, and Holland. We explored a little into Denmark and Sweden and then back through France. Finally, we drove around England a little bit more, returned the van, and flew home.

We began our adventure by flying out of Vancouver, taking the slow route across Canada. In those days you couldn't fly over the pole, so we had stop in Edmonton, Winnipeg, and Toronto, and finally ended up at Gatwick near London. Once we arrived, my cousin, who was studying at Oxford, met us at the airport and took us to pick up our van.

We all took turns driving. Driving on the opposite side of the road held challenges for us world travellers. We carefully pulled out of the lot where we had purchased the van, entered a roundabout, and got off on the wrong side of the road. Oncoming traffic raised our young heartbeats to 220 and a group meeting was immediately scheduled.

The first day we headed straight for Paris, taking the ferry. When we got to France we cruised up the coast. It was already quite late and we needed to go to the washroom so we decided to stop at this big casino, asking the maître d' at the door where the bathroom was in French. In Québec, the word "salle de bain" meant bathroom. In France, it meant the place where you take a bath. We didn't know we needed to ask for the "toilette." It took several misunderstandings before the maître d' understood. That was our first instance of not being able to speak proper French. High school French just didn't cut it over there.

We reached the Eiffel Tower after midnight. There was no one around, so we zoomed right up and parked underneath it. We set up our sleeping bags and closed all the windows and curtains. In the morning, we were awoken by pounding on our van. We were in the main parking lot and security was kicking us out.

Today, you couldn't get anywhere near that landmark. Back then, we got as close as we possibly could. We had a similar experience at the Leaning Tower of Pisa, arriving at night when the parking lot was empty, and driving right up beside it. Nowadays they build big areas around the site, with a lot more buildings and security where cars get stopped. No one can drive within two miles of any of these places. Europe has changed.

We spent a few days wandering around Paris marvelling at the detail on the buildings, the art nouveau Metro, the cafés, water buses, walking along the Seine and seeing the iron details on the bridges and streetlamps. We didn't drive too much because driving in Paris is crazy, especially with six lanes of traffic. If you get stuck in the middle lane and you need to make your way to the outside, you're out of luck. It's easy to get completely confused when there are eight different exits on a roundabout, so we took the Metro.

With the help of our broken French we figured out how to arrive at our destinations. We went to the Louvre, the Champs-Elysees, the Arc de Triomphe—all the main sites. At Notre-Dame Cathedral, we walked up two hundred stairs.

Years later, when I took my family to Paris when the kids were teenagers, they all wanted to climb the stairs in all the tallest churches and buildings so they could say they did it, and they got to see some spectacular views. They loved the

Eiffel Tower because it was such a world-renowned structure. It was exciting for my wife and I to see Europe through their eyes.

The French people were quite nice to us. My friends and I were walking along and stopped in this artistic, bohemian area where hippies were hanging out with their sketchpads, long hair, and love beads, and we bought some pizza. This girl came up and asked me for a bite. It was a different era, a different time. People were friendlier than they are now. But we didn't really meet many girls or hang out with them. We were a bunch of nerds.

Europe was awe-inspiring. We pretty much hit all the sites in every major city in Europe. From Paris we headed to Spain, through to Portugal and on to Barcelona. Somewhere near Barcelona we parked on the beach. We were always having these episodes where people were banging on our van. One morning, after being awakened by shouting and pounding, we opened the door and standing before us were men dressed in army uniforms with machine guns pointed at us. We were pretty scared that time. We'd never seen guns like that before.

They told us to get out and sit on the ground and then they searched the van, looking for drugs or some kind of illegal activity. We were too nerdy to have any drugs, so they let us go.

We went to a lot of pubs, especially in Germany, and tried out every single brewery we came across. In those days you had to take the official brewery tour to be served beer, and those tours were very, very popular—so popular, it required us to be there at 6:00 or 7:00 a.m. to get in line. We knew we could get a free meal at the breweries, so we'd take turns standing in line. Breakfast consisted of knockwurst and all the beer you could drink. Around noon, we'd emerge from the darkened interiors, totally plastered, with spots in our eyes from the sunshine.

The rest of the day we'd hang out people-watching at coffee shops in the squares. Mostly we would park somewhere and walk around and see the sights. Then we'd go to the pub again.

One day, we crossed over Checkpoint Charlie to see Communist East Berlin. It was so drab there. After you walk through the checkpoint, you were allowed to spend an hour or two. It was heavily armed and people were shot every once in a while trying to escape to West Berlin. West Berlin was lit up with neon lights, music, and bustling nightlife while East Berlin was such a dull contrast—nondescript, no big buildings, no lights, no entertainment, nothing going on really, at all.

One of the scariest things happened going back to West Berlin through the No Man's Land. We accidentally ended up on a ring road that took us towards Poland, still under communist control. Peter became very concerned when we saw a sign that said the Polish border was 20 kilometres ahead. His family had escaped Poland and he did not want to make explanations to the Polish border guards.

We made a quick U-turn in the middle of the road and luckily we were pulled over by a police car. The policeman was very stern with us. I'd never have thought getting a ticket was a good thing, but this time it worked in our favour.

When we arrived at the other side, the guards wanted to know why it took so long to reach West Berlin, and we had that ticket to prove that we'd gone the wrong way. We could've been in real trouble without that ticket. There was extra uneasiness and concern if you were North American or Western European visiting Communist countries. There was a lot more tension back then in all of Europe because of the Cold War.

So once again, we were searched and patted down. They searched the van, they searched underneath the van, they looked in the engine—they looked everywhere. Maybe it was our faces, or the fact that we were young, or five guys on the loose in Europe. For some reason we got searched a lot!

When we went to nightclubs in the major cities, they'd feature the same types of bands there that we had in North America. We were wondering what the music was going to be like, but they were copying a lot of what the Americans were doing, which was imitating the British Invasion, or American pop songs. You'd go into a bar there and you'd never know you weren't in Canada. Every band was covering the Beatles. It was all amazingly similar.

During the day you could see the differences in the way people were dressed. Some looked like Europeans—with woollen pants and baggy shirts and the individuated cuts of the clothes—older styles that people in the West weren't wearing anymore, but in the nightclubs, everyone dressed like Americans.

Today, when you go to Europe you can't tell the difference—everyone's wearing exactly the same clothing. In those days you could tell when someone was from Holland as opposed to being from Germany, and people from Germany dressed differently from people from France. Back then, there were distinguishing characteristics to the clothes, but not anymore.

I remember Dubrovnik, in Croatia, right on the Adriatic Sea, was just a beautiful city with stunning architecture. It was a joy to just wander around and look at the buildings. We were chased by some Gypsies along the coast, further down south toward Albania. They were on horses, waving swords and running around us. I think they were just having fun with us. We didn't know what they wanted, but they eventually went away. It was a secondary road on the map and so maybe we weren't supposed to be there.

We picked up three girls hitchhiking. Two of them were from Vancouver and one was from California. It was pretty crowded there in the van. Their fathers were judges for the Supreme Court. They were fun to joke around with and they chipped in for gas. We made it all the way down to Greece with them and we left them there.

In Greece, we spent most of our time on the beach on Mykonos relaxing by the water. It was so gorgeous there and the sea was crystal clear. Most of the time in the big cities we would spend about an hour walking around, but we would also try to spend time at the beach. There were so many things to see and we had such a short time to see everything.

We paid to park the van at one of the big hotels and flew to Israel, where we had a great time. There was just so much history to absorb. This ancient part of the world is awe-inspiring. In Vancouver the oldest building was thirty years old. Nothing's really old here in North America. Over there, some structures were thousands of years old, so you can't help but to be inspired by the human drama that has played out over the centuries right where you would be standing.

In Israel, we did a whirlwind tour with a tour group so we could see everything. I have been back once since then.

On that trip we saw the highlights in Jerusalem and Tel Aviv. Now everything there is built up with shops and restaurants all crowded together.

Everywhere you go in Europe is different now. Back then it was less touristy. You could go right into many of the little sites mentioned in the travel magazines as great places to visit. They were just open and anyone could wander in and take a look. Now there isn't a parking lot in Europe that you go to that you don't have to pay for. Back then a lot of it was free.

It's also more built up for the tourists. Nowadays a lot of what you see at the Roman Colosseum has been rebuilt, and back then it wasn't that way. When I went, there was only one section of wall left standing. Now they've reconstructed the whole thing.

I studied Latin for four years in school, so Roman history was pretty fresh in my mind, and with the Latin language background, I could basically look at words and figure them out because there are so many similarities between the root Latin and French, Italian, and Spanish.

That didn't help all that much with pharmacology, though. At the beginning of high school they told me I had to take Latin, and then by the time I finished they told me I didn't need to take Latin. But Latin is still a good base to have because you can put words together that you don't understand and figure them out. It wasn't just the language that was helpful; we also studied Homer and the *Odyssey* and *Iliad*, so that gave us a frame of reference for myths and stories talked about in the places we'd visit. And there were always references to Homer and his work in other classics we read.

We flew back from Israel to Greece, picked up the van, and drove up through Bulgaria, which was still Communist, stopping at a small roadside restaurant that was really a house with a few tables and chairs in the front. They served us a delicious lamb dinner with wine for about a dollar—fabulous home-cooked food, dirt cheap. In those days in Bulgaria, that little roadside place was considered a big restaurant. There wasn't much along the road. You could go for miles and miles and not see any houses.

Bulgaria had quite a lot of little villages and in the cities they had streetcars. It was quite pretty. Sofia was a lively city. In the northern part of Bulgaria we found a caretaker outside the city who took us on a tour of underground caves where the stalactites were still intact—incredible and very distinctive. The caves we visited in Greece were very deep but weren't complete with original stalactites. The Bulgarian guides cautioned us not to talk about where we were going and what we were doing. I think they thought we were spies. Those dictatorships were tightly run and Bulgaria was part of the Soviet Union back then.

We would tip these guys, and basically anyone who helped us. All they wanted was a few bucks so they could buy parts for their cars. If they had American money, they could buy American parts. So they toured us around and we gave them some cash. It was a great deal for all of us.

We went nightclubbing there, wondering if we'd hear some authentic cultural music, but again it consisted of loud American or British rock 'n' roll and people dressed as if they were trying to look like Americans, even in Bulgaria!

We toured the northern European countries and later in the summer we spent a lot of our trip in Amsterdam, where it stayed light longer in the evening.

I don't remember Denmark all that well. It was bustling and we went to a big circus in the middle of town, a year-long event, and to some of the major sites like the parliament building in the capital, Copenhagen. Driving was out of the question because we couldn't read the signs. Our method was to drive as close to downtown as possible in the big cities and then walk the rest of the way in and pick up walking maps. A lot of people spoke English so they would give us directions.

Circling back to where we started, we toured Scotland and saw the major sites around London, and finally returned the van. When I went with my family to England later on, we spent time in the London museums but also were able to see more of the countryside, driving through rolling green hills and spotting the castles, fortresses, and huge manor houses.

After five months of sleeping in a van with four other people, Ken Garfinkel and Peter Kafka are still two of my closest friends. By the time we left Europe, everyone was getting pretty sad and homesick. It was great to soak up so much history, but when you're away for that length of time, it's wonderful to get back home again too. We had all had enough travelling by then.

Whenever I'd go back to the places we visited, I would try to remember what it looked like back in 1970. That trip opened my eyes and made me more aware of all the different ways people live their lives, all the styles and customs and cultures. It was life changing. It altered how I see the world. It made me more open and accepting of other ways of life.

I feel so fortunate to have taken that trip when I could. A lot of people never get to travel like that. I run into Americans my age who have never been outside America—they've never even been to Canada. They don't understand why they would even need a passport. Travelling has definitely expanded my horizons.

# Chapter Eight

## Calculating My Future

I n the fall of 1970, after my Europe trip, I took an unclassified year at the university just to raise my marks. Before then, I'd been scraping through, so I deliberately took easier courses to get accepted into the pharmacy school: Ethnology, Human Genetics, Sociology, Abnormal Psychology, and Group Psychology, and they all did the trick—they brought my marks up.

But not as much as one of my psychology courses, where I actually received a grade of one hundred percent. The teacher was a nice lady, a little Jewish woman from New York. She couldn't get along with the head of the department, and near the end of the semester, they fired her, so she gave everyone the highest grade she could. Everyone got a perfect grade. She was a hippie and didn't fit in with the typical tweedy psychology professors, but she sure did make it easier for me to reach my goal!

When I started pharmacy school the following year, it wasn't easy. I was having so much trouble with difficult calculations in Chemistry. I didn't have the background in logarithms, natural logarithms, and other technical long equations.

Edging into my third year of pharmacy, I was enrolled in a course entailing many calculations for the half-life of drugs. The trouble with these calculations is they are either perfect down to the fifth decimal or they are totally wrong. You could get the main numbers right, but way down after the decimal point have one number out of place and still you'd get a zero grade. I could either get one hundred or zero, never a middle-ground mark for being partially right.

This was giving me a lot of anxiety, when, in the summer of 1972, I was skimming through a scientific magazine I read every once in a while and there was an article about some new handheld scientific calculators coming onto the market. This particular one was manufactured by Commodore, selling for under two hundred dollars. That was a lot of money in those days, but if you were in pharmacy school having trouble with your calculations, you'd pay that amount if you were as desperate as I was.

Off I went to the Commodore dealer on Seymour Street, where they sold office supplies, desks, and filing cabinets. I showed the owner the article and asked if he could order me one of those calculators. He said he would. He called me later and said he could place an order, but the minimum order was one hundred.

One hundred calculators at the retail price of $199 would be almost $20,000, but if I bought them wholesale they'd cost $99 each—that meant $10,000! Where was I going to get $10,000? But I had to have one, so I showed all my friends the article and asked if they would buy one.

Pretty much everyone I talked to said they would, so I was convinced I could sell one hundred calculators.

I rushed downtown to see one of my relatives, Uncle Harvey, a mining engineer. I showed him the article and told him I needed ten thousand dollars. He quizzed me for a while to make sure I was certain I could sell all one hundred calculators. I had to be very careful with my words around him—he was a no-nonsense businessman and he was the only person I knew with that much money. But when Sheldon needed his first car, Uncle Harvey managed to come up with one for him. He came off as being gruff, but he really had a big heart.

I sat there for a moment thinking about it one more time. I was taking a big risk. Students said they wanted a calculator, but when it came to forking over the cash would they really come through? Then again, without that calculator, how could I get through pharmacy school?

So I told Uncle Harvey I was certain I could sell every last one of those calculators, and that everyone I talked to wanted one. He agreed to loan me the money, and he walked to the bank across the street with a piece of gold to use as collateral.

That nugget of gold came from his gold mine on Vancouver Island. Harvey's workers would blast for gold, fill a truck full of ore, and have it hauled to the refinery, where it would be turned into bricks of gold. It wasn't a huge mine. It was a two- or three-man operation, and it wasn't the only business he was involved with, but whatever gold they could squeeze out of it, they kept.

Harvey also flew a helicopter. During World War II, he was in the tank corps, stationed in Manitoba at a big training facility, teaching soldiers how to operate and fix tanks. Then he worked at the Britannia Mine, which has been totally redone today and is offering tours. Back in his day, it was only accessible by boat.

Harvey was very creative and figured out how to accomplish his goals. To find gold, he flew airplanes with magnetic sensors covering huge areas at a time, searching for minerals under the ground.

I took Uncle Harvey's ten thousand dollars to the dealer and ordered the calculators. When they arrived from California, I took pictures of them and had some flyers made up to be ready when the new school year started.

When people registered at UBC for their courses, they were given a little computer card for each course. I was taking six courses, so I needed six computer cards. It was a time-consuming event, running run back and forth to each booth to make sure you enrolled in all the classes you wanted.

One hundred students were let in at a time, first-come first-served, and it was bedlam. There was a huge line out the front door. Once students handed in all of their computer cards, they'd leave through the back door, and there I was with my flyers. I'd made ten thousand flyers selling the calculators for $149. I split the difference. I figured I could sell them more quickly at $149 than $199. At that time you couldn't even get them in any store. I think I had the first batch!

There was a lot of buzz and tons of excitement that day, so I bought an answering machine because I couldn't be home taking calls all the time. Back then, it was a great big box with reel-to-reel tapes. Returning home the first day, the machine was completely full.

I returned all those phone calls, telling buyers to meet me in the pharmacy lounge the next day and bring cash, and I sold all one hundred calculators in two days; students were lined up and down the hall. I made about fifteen thousand dollars, so I'd be able to pay my uncle back his money.

I ordered another hundred calculators. People were still calling me and looking for me in the lounge. I received the new shipment the following week and sold them quickly.

I put in a third order and tried a fourth, but they wouldn't allow me to order them because the product had gone so stratospheric, the rest of North America wanted it too. I think the US campuses started a week later than we did, so that gave me a head start.

They could not make those calculators fast enough. I begged them to send them to me, and I phoned California and offered them cash. I spoke to the head person at the factory. He told me about a company called Melcor in Farmington, New York. Their new calculator did the same things and would be coming off the line the following week. I phoned that company and, sure enough, they had them in production. They told me to send the cash and they'd get them out to me.

I ordered one hundred calculators from Melcor to start with. They were a little different, but pretty much the same concerning all the necessary functions. I went through many orders from Melcor before they couldn't meet my supply either.

The calculators were used in all sorts of scientific classes: chemistry, physics, and engineering, not just the pharmacy school, and I was able to sell a bunch of Hewlett Packards to the engineers. The Hewlett Packards in Canada were tightly regulated. They could only be sold out of one outlet in Vancouver. One of the engineers actually phoned me and wanted a special Hewlett Packard that was programmable; it was actually the first programmable calculator ever, and he wanted me to get him a good deal on it.

Western Washington University in Bellingham was selling those HPs in their bookstore and they gave me a deal. I made about 20 percent and split that with the engineers. They gave me an order for approximately five hundred of these calculators, but they were expensive—about four hundred dollars each.

Then I started selling Texas Instruments. I dabbled in that, but most of my profit came from the early Commodores where I made fifty dollars apiece. By October, my profit margin had dropped and the market was pretty well saturated. I wasn't taking any more orders, so I closed up shop. All told, I earned about thirty thousand dollars in profit.

I'd been so busy selling calculators, that I didn't do any schoolwork. One of my professors called me and warned me that if I didn't catch up I would flunk out. I hadn't even handed in one assignment. After that, I started applying myself and got down to work.

To make up for taking over the Pharmacy Student Lounge for my calculator business, I offered to pay for all the drinks at the Pharmacy graduation party. After I graduated I bought a parcel of land in Richmond with the calculator money. The vacant lot was worth $30,000 then. Today that same lot with the house on it is worth more than a million dollars. To give you an idea, in those days a gallon of gas was 25 cents and it's $5 now. So $30,000 then would be the equivalent of $600,000 in today's money.

We have lived in the same house we built on that property in 1976. It's been wonderful for our kids because it's the only home they've ever known. They were able to attend the same schools and feel well grounded. They didn't ever have to worry about changing schools and making new friends.

I bought a large enough lot that we could expand on it. We started out with a 2,000 square-foot house and now have a 3,200 square-foot house. Here I am living in a beautiful home in a great neighbourhood that's worth a million dollars, all because I happened to read an article in a magazine. I just had a feeling it would work out, and following my hunches has served me well, creating a solid foundation for my career and family life.

# Chapter Nine
## Meeting My Wife

During pharmacy school I met my future wife. It was in 1970 when I first saw Barb with another guy at a party. I noticed her across the room right away and I was smitten. Barb was small with long, long hair. Her small stature was appealing to me because I'm not that tall. Barb looked like the perfect girl next door. She was pleasant and smiled all the time.

There were some candles burning and some wax spilled on her leg. I went over to help pick off the wax, and the guy she was with wasn't too happy about that. He was double my size, so my friend said I was lucky he wasn't that interested in her or there could have been a fight. But this guy didn't make a big deal of it; it was obvious Barb and I were attracted to each other. We started dating, however for her it was just dating and nothing serious. But I wanted to be more than friends.

Barb and I dated for six years before we got married. I asked her out many times in the first six months. She was attending nursing school and my friends and I would study at the hospital library and pop into their cafeteria during coffee breaks to search for the nurses we were interested in. This place also happened to be close to the pub, so we didn't get as much studying done as we should have.

I told Sheldon, "I met a girl at the hospital library," when I met the love of my life. Sometimes Barb and I would double date with Sheldon and his girlfriend Debbie, who became his wife. Barb worked until eleven p.m. and Sheldon worked until ten-thirty or eleven, so midnight was when our evening started. Then we'd go out until two or three in the morning. There were a few restaurants that were still open and we'd go for coffee and talk or see a late movie. Sheldon got married to Debbie in 1973. Bonnie was only 12 years old when I met Barb, but now they are very good friends.

I liked Barb's easy-going nature and we got along very well. I would do anything for her; people could tell I was smitten with her. Barb finally decided that it was going to work out with us. It took us about five or six months to become romantically involved, then we started seeing each other regularly.

After a few years, we knew we wanted to stay together, but Barb wasn't Jewish; in fact, her parents were staunch Catholics. That was a bit of a problem, so there was a little hesitation there. They didn't mind me, but they didn't really want me marrying their daughter either.

Barb and I dated for about six years because I wanted to get through school before we got married. We started planning to get married in 1975—that's when I graduated from pharmacy school. Our wedding was planned for May 23, 1976. Barb's parents were a bit hesitant about her rejecting her Catholic upbringing, but she had an aunt who was a nun—a very progressive nun. Her aunt came to me and wanted to talk. She could see that we were set on getting married and decided if it was meant to be, it was meant to be. She spoke with Barb's parents and they decided that becoming Jewish did not mean that she would become a different person and they looked at things with a more open-minded attitude. My mother had accepted rather quickly that Barb was Catholic. There was no real problem with it. Eventually, Barb converted, so we ended up having a Jewish wedding in a synagogue on Tenth Avenue. It was a very small congregation and they had to rent out the Legion Hall to hold their services, so that's where the wedding was held. There were about one hundred people at the wedding, including relatives from Winnipeg, Vancouver, Ottawa, and some Americans too. We had people from all over. Luckily I had the money to pay for it because of those calculators!

## Honeymoon

On our honeymoon we decided to drive across Canada for five weeks. Barb thought it would be nice to go to Hawaii and stay in fancy hotels and lie around and do nothing, but now she agrees that our honeymoon was fun and different, and we stopped along the way to meet some relatives. We rented an Econoline van with a bed in the back and a little propane stove. We were in a confined space for five weeks in the back of the van, so we really got to know each other! We used that as a camper and went all the way across Canada. We stayed at Lake Louise, went to Winnipeg, Ontario, Montréal, and then over to Nova Scotia.

We went part of the way back to Vancouver taking the American route. We toured Maine, Connecticut, New York, and Minnesota. We went south of the Great Lakes, coming up by Lake Superior, and then went back through Canada. We saw so many different kinds of geography—prairies and mountains and lakes—everything. We also went to Niagara Falls. We saw Banff and Jasper and experienced all the different touristy things, including the huge mountains in Jasper, with the ice fields in summer. It was beautiful and awe inspiring for us.

We had a canoe on the roof of the van tied down with straps. We went through a canyon and up a steep hill and when we reached the crest of the hill, the wind blew up under the boat and broke the strap. Our canoe came crashing down onto the road where it was promptly run over by the truck behind me, smashing into four or five pieces.

When the policeman showed up, he wanted to give me a ticket for not securing the boat properly. I told him we were on our honeymoon and he gave us a warning. We had pulled over to the side of the road and so did the truck driver, who turned out to be quite a nice man. He picked up the pieces of the canoe and took it back to Vancouver for us, but I wasn't able to fix it.

## Starting Our Family

Barb and I got married in May and started building our house in September, and were finished by December. It was exciting to choose everything—all the different colours, the furniture, the carpets, the appliances. There were a couple rooms we didn't even open because we had electric heat and it was expensive. It was about two thousand square feet at the time it was built and we had moved from a very small apartment. Eventually we built two additions, as we had more children. We closed in an open loft above the living room to make another bedroom. Then later on we added another two bedrooms above the garage and another couple of bathrooms.

Before we were married, Barb and I had talked about having children. We were married three years before we had our first child, Alisa, in 1979. When we discovered we were having a baby, we were very excited. We didn't know we were having a girl in advance—we wanted to be surprised, and we were, with all four of our kids. They say it's bad luck to know the sex ahead of time. That's a superstition, but still we liked not knowing until the birth of our children.

Our first two children were born at Vancouver General Hospital, where Barb worked as an RN. We went in the night before Alisa's birth, and it was a long, long labour. I was in the room with Barb for the delivery. The first time I held Alisa in my arms, it was so intense, the love I felt. I cried, I was so grateful. My mother was in the waiting room, anxious to see her new grandchild.

Your first child is always special. We really wanted a girl. Barb wanted girls because she knew our kids would be short. Alisa is barely 5 feet tall, Jeffrey and Craig are about 5' 4", and Kevin is the really tall one at 5' 9", and he was the smallest baby.

We had a little incident with Alisa when she was two. She was at a party next door, eating carrots. She started crying for some reason, and as she came running home, she aspirated a piece of carrot and part of her lung collapsed. At that time, Barb was pregnant with Jeffrey and actually delivered the baby at the same time Alisa was in the hospital. I was running back and forth between two different wings. That was in 1981.

While Alisa's birth was without incident, Jeffrey had the umbilical cord wrapped around his neck. That was scary.

They ordered me out of the room and all the different doctors came in to push the baby back in and get the cord off. It only took a few minutes but it seemed like forever. It was very emotional.

The next baby was Kevin, born in 1984 at Women's Hospital. The evening he was born, Barb and I were taking the kids to the nearby park when her water broke. I rushed home to get the car, picked them all up from the park, dropped the kids off at my mother's, and we sped off to the hospital. His birth was much easier than Jeffrey's, and he was born a few hours after our arrival.

When we found out Barb was pregnant with the fourth baby, we were a little surprised, but really happy. As Barb says, having two kids takes all your time, three takes all your time, and four takes all your time—it doesn't matter how many you have. With Craig, born in 1986, the birth took only about an hour. Shortly after arriving at the hospital, we were left alone in the delivery room. Craig decided to announce his arrival, so I called for help and the nurse and I delivered him together. It was a pretty amazing experience.

Alisa didn't mind having three brothers, most of the time. They got along pretty well, but she always wished she had a sister. She was closest to Craig. He was like her little doll since he was the youngest, and she used to dress him up in dresses, necklaces and pigtails.

Just like me, the boys weren't heavily into team sports as kids, but they all played baseball and shared my love for skiing. It worked out well because we didn't have to travel much for baseball, as they were all on local teams. I took the kids skiing many times over the years and when my grandkids were old enough I started taking them too. One time on the mountain with his friends, Craig had an incident where he fell down and dislocated his shoulder. It got so bad that he eventually had to have surgery and hasn't been boarding for four or five years now. All my kids enjoy the outdoors, like me.

When our children were young, we took them on many weekend trips to the campgrounds in BC. The British Columbia Scouting organization has a lot of land in BC. Regardless of which group you are affiliated with, you could use any of the land owned by the Scouts. So there were a variety of places where we could go. We mostly went out toward Harrison where there were some hot springs near the Hemlock Valley ski area. It was beautiful, wooded, and had a small waterfall, with hiking trails on both sides of the road. I took our kids up to the ski hill one spring when there was still some snow left, and we all went sliding.

## The Family Tree Grows

My children's Bat and Bar Mitzvah's were very exciting milestones in our lives. Alisa's was the first, and she studied very hard in grade seven to prepare to lead the services, to read from the Torah and write a speech. We had a big party at the house, and a large family brunch at the country club on the weekend. Alisa also got together with another girl from Hebrew school and had a party with all of their friends at a hall. It was really exciting and a lot of fun for them. While not many kids really enjoy going to Hebrew school, having a Bar or Bat Mitzvah and making a connection to the Jewish community made it worthwhile for my kids. As children, most of their Jewish friends were from Hebrew school, but they also made many friends from Washington and Oregon while going to Camp Solomon Schechter in Olympia, Washington.

Alisa was very into sports in high school. She was actually great at basketball even though she was just barely five feet tall. She loved dribbling and dodging around the other girls. Because of her basketball skills, excelling at school activities and her schoolwork, Alisa earned the Best All-Round Student award in grade twelve.

Alisa got a degree from UBC in English Literature and is a teacher now. She works with students who have difficulties keeping up, who have special needs, or who are learning English. She also teaches music. They don't have a full-time music teacher at that school, so she and another teacher fill that role. Alisa studied piano until she graduated from high school. She doesn't have much time to play now with two small children and a part-time teaching job, but I hope she goes back to playing again. She was very good.

Alisa met her husband, Marc Magnan, working for a contracting company in Vancouver before she got her teaching degree. He was from Edmonton and they enjoyed their work conversations so much, they decided to meet in person. He came to Vancouver to visit and they hit it off, eventually flying back and forth between Edmonton and Vancouver a couple times a month. He moved to Vancouver and was living in the lower suite of my mother's house until they got engaged. Like Barb, he was Catholic and decided to convert to Judaism. Both of our families were accepting of his conversion and they were married in 2004. They had their first daughter, Aviva, in 2008, and the second, Zoey, in 2011.

Our son Jeffrey was really enthusiastic about Scouts, just as I was. He went from Cubs all the way up through Rovers.

We always had the ratio of one adult leader to five kids, and there were about twenty kids in our troop.

In 1993 Jeffrey and I were headed to the Canadian Scouting jamboree in Kananaskis, Alberta, in a tour bus with about fifty or sixty people. Parents were in a van behind them with all the sleeping bags and other gear. Our van stopped for gas and when we came around a bend, we saw the Scouts' bus. At first we thought it was an odd place to park, but the closer we got, we realized that the bus was actually on its side. The driver had been driving for too long, over the limit he was supposed to drive, and he fell asleep. The bus went off the road and landed in a ditch.

They were lucky it happened there because anywhere else along the road would have been a half-mile drop. One Scout was injured because he was in the bathroom when it crashed. We had to get everyone out of there quickly and the police came to the scene. But we still had to wait for the next bus to drive to the jamboree camp, unload their group, and come back for Jeff, me, and all the other kids—a four- or five-hour trip. We don't know what ever happened to the bus driver. It never hit the papers. It was early in the morning, quiet, and he just dozed off. It could have been way worse.

The jamboree was Canada-wide and fighter jets flew over for the opening ceremony. There were thousands of kids there, over acres of land in Kananaskis. Each day they had different activities. I remember we made chains out of wood and we silkscreened T-shirts. So many activities all week long, meeting so many people—it was really a great time.

Jeffrey has my entrepreneurial spirit and he likes to fix things and do things around the house like me. He's working for the company that bought my nursing home business.

Jeffrey was managing that part of the business already, so he stayed with that company when I sold it. He's in charge of getting new business and promotions and he's building the business so he doesn't have to run it out of one location anymore. Sheldon calls him Marvin number two because he thinks Jeffrey is the most like me. He also has a Bachelor of Science degree from UBC.

Jeff married Elizabeth Elperin in 2005, almost a year to the day after Alisa and Marc were married. They met at UBC, like Barb and I. Their children are: Yosef, born in 2007; Ephraim, born in 2010; Sari, born in 2011; and they have a baby on the way.

Kevin takes after me in that he's interested in technology. He's more like my father was, a little more passive, more easygoing, not a type-A personality at all. He really liked to play computer games as a boy, especially SimCity. He loved online games so much it was hard to drag him away from his computer. He took courses recently to upgrade his classes so he could get a job in software engineering. He has a degree in political science and a bachelor of computer science. He's been working at a non-profit organization in Seattle.

I remember when Kevin was young and we were visiting my sister, Bonnie, in Edmonton. We went to the West Edmonton Mall, the largest shopping mall in North America. Kevin saw all these coins in the fountain and he walked right into it to pick them up—and he slipped and fell. He was about two years old then and to this day Alisa and Jeffrey still give him a hard time about it.

Kevin did some Scouting with me as well, but he dropped out because two of the groups were amalgamated and the newly merged group had very strong leaders already. I wasn't really welcome to stay, so wasn't a part of Kevin's Scouting anymore. I think that's one of the reasons he lost interest. When Kevin left Scouting, he took up tae kwon do. He had been a quiet kid, and he wanted to be a little more aggressive. He was very good at it and earned a couple of belts. Kevin married Robin, his long-time camp girlfriend, in 2007 and they have a little boy, Daniel, who was born in 2010.

Being the youngest, Craig looked up to his siblings, wanting to do what they were doing—playing baseball because his brothers and sister were doing it, joining all the Jewish youth groups, going to Jewish camp—he even joined the Jewish fraternity because of his brothers.

Craig really liked being in Cubs with me too. He was always a very shy boy, and he didn't want to go through Beavers without me, so he waited until the next year to do Cubs and Scouts with his dad. We really enjoyed camping together with the Scouts. There was a big campsite on the Sunshine Coast, Camp Byng. It had a huge lodge with a well-equipped kitchen and the Scouts could sleep inside the lodge, rather than in the tents, when it was raining.

There's a nice old rustic cabin at the bottom of Cypress Mountain ski hill that's been in the Scout's possession for years. It's about seventy-five years old, a big A-frame. All the kids sleep upstairs in the "A." There was a kitchen on the main floor. It was a bit cramped but it was great for outpost hiking, and you could rent snowshoes up there too. All of the cabins are at least fifty years old. No one is allowed to build up there anymore; there's a moratorium on any more structures so it's not too crowded, and it's really charming.

Craig started playing Ultimate Frisbee in grade eight because Jeff was playing and he discovered he had a real passion for it. I was always worrying that he would get injured.

He asked me for so many ankle braces and ThermoFlow wraps for his injuries. He played Ultimate for fourteen years before I finally came to watch one of his games. He was so happy I was there. I finally realized how much he loved it and stopped bugging him to quit playing.

Craig has a certificate in Film and Video and he's dabbled in acting too. I let him use my camera to make short videos with his friend Steve. Later he joined the A/V club in high school, and he also played the drums for a couple of years in a band called Valmont, named after the street where I owned a warehouse where they practiced.

Craig also has a diploma in business management from Kwantlen Polytechnic University, which he earned while working at Coastlines Fashions, an import/export clothing company. He pretty much runs the place himself, a one-man show. He's like me in that he's adventurous. He's really come into his own and I'm so proud of him.

Craig is the only one in the family who is unmarried. He does have a long-term girlfriend, Krystle Eng, and they will probably get married one day. Recently, Craig and I had a talk about how difficult it is for him that I won't be there to meet and play with his children someday, since now I know my days are numbered.

All in all, my kids each have a calm demeanour like their parents. All of our children have our sarcastic sense of humour as well, and we all engage in some pretty silly jokes that we like to tell over and over.

## Our Family Vacations

We took the kids on several trips in Canada and the US. We visited the Northwest Territories—where Sheldon and his kids lived—once in the 1990s, in the summer when the roads were good and it was daytime all night. The kids got to hang out with their cousins, Joel and Mandy. Although it was permanent sunlight, the sun wasn't really all that bright; it just sort of hovered on the horizon. There was so little grass there and the trees were only two feet tall. In the winter it could get as cold as forty below, and you would have to wear something on your eyes so they wouldn't freeze when you went outside.

When the kids were little, we made trips to Disney World and Disneyland. It was March when we went to Disney World for spring break, and it became very stormy. One day we were in the wave pool and it was super hot, and the next day it was so cold and pouring rain. Disney World emptied out and we were practically the only ones there.

Luckily I have a cousin who lives in Fort Lauderdale who was driving up with her husband in their motor home to meet us. They had some warm clothing, extra sweaters and jackets. It was really a freak storm. Limbs of trees and signs were blowing down. It was like that for the rest of the week. There were no lines for the rides—especially the water rides—so our kids were able to get off a ride and hop back on another ride. We went to Disneyland twice. When we first drove there, Craig was only two, in 1988.

Another driving trip involved visiting my friend in Santa Fe. We drove all the way down from Vancouver and toured Bryce Canyon in Utah; saw the north side of the Grand Canyon, and the pueblos where the Anasazis built cities into cliffs in New Mexico. We took hikes through those rugged red spires and then drove up the winding road following the Rio Grande to Taos. We did some camping and some motel, and the kids had a lot of fun.

The trip lasted about three weeks. Alisa kept a list each day of which state we were in and how many states we went through—thirteen states altogether. This was before DVD players, so the kids played travel games. They didn't have little screens on their phones or portable video games. They had to amuse themselves somehow, and that included arguing.

We were riding in one of the first minivans that featured captain's chairs in the second row and the kids were always fighting over who got to sit in them. I actually had to make a seating plan because everyone wanted to sit in the captain's chairs, but certain people didn't want to sit next to each other. It caused so many arguments that Barb and I had to enforce a rotational seating plan.

The hotels would charge extra if there were more than four people in a room, so we usually didn't tell them there were six of us. We would go to a hotel to get a room, and two kids would stay in the car. We'd check in, saying there were four people total, come back out and then the other two would sneak into the room, and some of them would sleep on the floor in sleeping bags.

We saw the Grand Canyon, which was magnificent, with the storms coming up over the canyon so suddenly and the red variegated cliffs with the Colorado River snaking through way below us. We visited Monument Valley in Utah, with the gorgeous spires, buttes, and crimson rock. In Monument Valley we were able to stay in a campground on top of a hill and see in every direction for miles around us, but now they have moved all the camping to the valley floor. We also toured Zion National Park and Yellowstone Park, with the volcanic geysers and Old Faithful. We went to the Four Corners, where you can stand in four states at once. We did so much camping and hiking. That was a memorable trip and the kids settled down once they could climb out of the car, get some exercise, and be in nature.

Our kids have grown up being exposed to camping, Scouting, sports, hiking, and all sorts of activities. Because I have the travel bug, they've grown to love it too. Barb enjoys it as well, as long as I organize it!

# Chapter Ten

## Pharmacy Beginnings

I graduated from UBC in 1975 and got a job at Fedco, a small department store with a pharmacy inside. One of my friends had a cousin who was involved with a company placing pharmacies in department stores, including the larger Fedco stores, and they were looking for three pharmacy managers. My friend asked me if I wanted the position, and I was happy to accept. Unfortunately, the Fedco stores didn't do very well, only lasting about a year because London Drugs dominated the marketplace. After Fedco went out of business, I worked at London Drugs for about seven years as a pharmacist and pharmacy manager.

### The Clock Biz

When I was with London Drugs, they had a program called Junior Achievement, allowing high school kids to get a little taste of business. The teens were divided into groups. Two or three adults would be in charge of each group, teaching school kids how to run their own businesses. We would help them with an idea for a product, and how to make the product, sell it, and then market it, so they would learn what it's like to have a real business.

One year we came up with the idea of making clocks. We ordered ceramic tiles and the plastic numbers and drilled the holes for the clock parts. Then we put them together. We had a successful little company that year.

After Junior Achievement was over, I continued making clocks and I looked for a source for larger quantities of clock parts. This was about the time miniature clock movements came out; the centre was about 1½-x-1-inch thick. Before that, they were about double that size and used a large C battery. The new movements used a double A battery, so they had come down in size quite a bit. I found a source in Toronto first, and eventually started buying them directly from Japan for about a dollar each.

I began to make clocks out of burled wood with smoothed resin on it, in addition to plastic and tile faces. I had the idea to put drug company logos on the clocks, created a prototype for a company called Novopharm, and silkscreened their logo on the clock. We sold about ten thousand clocks to Novopharm.

We had the whole family with the clocks lined up around the table and the grandparents and kids sitting around putting on the numbers and the hands, placing them in the boxes and sealing them. We made an extra five to ten thousand dollars a year making these clocks and had some fun doing it together.

I used to advertise in a weekly newspaper that was available across Canada. For one hundred dollars you could place an ad in one hundred papers, and for five hundred dollars you could run the ad in five hundred papers. I was getting orders from all over Canada. If you lived in northern Alberta and you wanted a clock part, how did you find out where to buy it? These little papers got read over and over because that's the only newspaper they had to read in some of the more remote areas. Those ads generated a lot of requests for our catalogues—every day we would get twenty or thirty requests.

In 1986, after a successful few years, I sold the clock business. After a while, the clock parts were easier to acquire and business slowed down. It's so much easier now to locate products on the Internet. Things are always changing, and knowing when to exit an enterprise is just as valuable as knowing when to jump into one.

## Marks' Plaza Pharmacy

I left London Drugs in 1981 when I took over my Uncle Harry's business. He was a pharmacist who had several nursing homes as customers. He had already sold his retail store and was ready to sell the nursing home business so I took it over.

I leased some office space on Cambie Street and moved the nursing home business over there. Eventually a pharmacy, called Marks' Plaza Pharmacy, became available for sale a few blocks away. The pharmacy was located in a large medical building, so I bought it and moved my whole operation over there. I had room to run the nursing home business in the back and the pharmacy in the front. It was a good location and I did an excellent volume of business over the next two decades. I sold that pharmacy recently, in 2010.

Jeffrey remembers that growing up, being in the pharmacy was something special. During the summers Alisa and Jeffrey would come to work with me, with my mother running the cash register. They would scratch lottery tickets, help package pills in the back, and other odd jobs. They really enjoyed it, and made a little bit of money, and they liked being around their dad and grandmother. There was a coffee shop below the pharmacy, so they would sometimes get a glazed doughnut in the morning. At the end of the day they would ask if they could get a treat, usually Maynards wine gums, and we would share it on the ride home.

My mother retired at sixty-five from her job at the synagogue and then came to work for me. She was a fast learner. I had a very early Linux computer system for the store, but she learned to use it to keep my books. Imagine, she was over sixty-five and she would pay all the bills. She was so dedicated that she had a second bedroom at her place that she turned into an office to keep all the ledger books and files.

She taught Alisa and Jeffrey how to run the register and sell lottery tickets. Whenever she was counting money or running the cash register, there were always a large number of Chinese customers coming in, and she learned how to greet them and say "thank you" in both Mandarin and Cantonese dialects. When Chinese New Year came around, in late January or February, she would greet people by saying "Happy New Year" to everyone in Chinese: "Kung Hei Fat Choy!"

When we first entered the nursing home business, we used bingo-type cards with thirty-five little holes called "blisters" for packaging the pills. They were foil-backed and secured with a heat sealer. The patient simply punched their pills through the foil.

I wasn't satisfied with that design so I created my own, approaching a company in Toronto that manufactured packaging for Coca-Cola. I had them make the blisters for me and ran my own line of blister cards that I sold to other pharmacists.

I eventually invented a plastic system that could be reused. The company's Toronto representative came to Vancouver to see me. They made a similar system for other products, so it wasn't much of a stretch to make a new die and reformulate the sizes. I just gave them the sketch and they did a great job of making the right size.

I was selling the system to other nursing homes, making money, and also increasing my own volume. Once the press was set up, the additional cards didn't cost me anything. If I could run an order of one hundred thousand or a million cards at a time, it was much cheaper than ordering a smaller volume.

I've always tried to improve on things, to come at things everyone takes for granted from a different angle, and most of my improvements and innovations have actually been successful.

Nursing homes, though, did not turn out to be as profitable as we thought. The trouble was that the government decided to pay a fixed rate for drugs. So no matter how many prescriptions were filled, we only made ten dollars per bed. If we had one hundred beds, we would still earn ten dollars per bed, even if every person needed multiple prescriptions. It wouldn't work out very well if you were totally dependent on it for your livelihood.

The government was pretty smart in fixing the numbers. It meant that patients wouldn't be overly medicated, and it kept health care costs down in Canada. This system is not common at all in the United States. When they do have a fixed fee per bed in the States, it's always a higher fee than ours. Even in the US, they still get paid per prescription. If they fill a pack of pills every week, they get a fee every week, so it can be very profitable—a weekly fee rather than a monthly fee.

Now there are new machines that package one week's worth of prescription medicine at a time in little cellophane packs. These are now almost universal in Canada. Every pharmacy needs that machine or the nursing homes won't deal with them. We also sell forms such as doctors' order sheets, printing them up in bigger numbers so it's cheaper to order from us. My brother-in-law Mel runs that part of my business from a warehouse in Richmond that I purchased around 1990.

I was one of the first to have a large packaging machine. They cost about $350,000 and can be interfaced with the pharmacy software. I purchased a used machine to package the prescriptions for the nursing homes and one of the generic companies financed it so that we would buy all our drugs from them.

After filling the prescriptions, the machine spits out little cellophane packages with the required drugs in each packet. Whatever the person takes with breakfast is in one packet, along with the name of each prescription drug and the patient's name, all printed right on the cellophane bag. The nurse just opens the bag and gives it to the patient. There are very few errors this way.

With our system we had a scanner that works with the Electronic Medication Administration Record (eMAR). All the packs were printed with bar codes. We would give the nursing home a laptop and a scanner and the nurse would not have to initial each time she gave a medication. She could just sign in, scan the packets, and her initials appeared automatically. If the nurse missed one, the program would start beeping as a reminder.

In the US most of the bigger and better hospitals have these scanners because they help them keep track of the drugs the patients are taking. If you scan a packet, and there in front of you is a different patient, it will tell you right away you are giving meds to the wrong patient. And for billing purposes it's great. If the patient needs a Tylenol, the nurse grabs it from the box, scans it, enters it, and the patient is billed for the Tylenol.

Pharmacists had to get in on the ground floor with the packaging or they'd be too late. It was another case of me plunging ahead and being glad I was an early adopter of new technology. In 2012, I sold the nursing home business to a large company from Ontario. It proved profitable to spend so many years building up the business and making it attractive enough to sell to a large corporation.

## President of the College of Pharmacists of BC

I was elected president of the College of Pharmacists of British Columbia in 1989. I ran for president of the council and served for two years, after one year as vice president, from 1988 to 1989. It was a real eye-opener to see how little influence the councillors have on the day-to-day operation of the college and the inspectors.

In one instance, a pharmacist was producing Mycostatin capsules for some physicians in the US. They would fax or mail him the prescription and he would mail the capsules to the patient. The physicians wanted pure Mycostatin only in their capsules, with none of the additives needed to make large quantities of tablets.

There was a strike by the post office so the pharmacist wasn't able to mail the capsules from Canada, so he took a batch of prescriptions across the border at Point Roberts, Washington, and mailed them from the US post office. Customs officers were unfamiliar with the drug, so they confiscated every bit of it, and his car as well.

After a few days they decided that the pharmacist had a prescription from an American doctor and it was only an antifungal, which could not be abused, so the American agents gave the car and products back to the pharmacist. The Canadian border officials felt he was not breaking any Canadian laws, so they let him back into Canada. They did contact the Health Protection Branch and they too were not interested in pursuing any charges.

The file was sent to the College of Pharmacists of BC to see if there was any interest in the case. The college lawyer felt that even though Mycostatin is an innocuous drug, prescriptions are technically only legal if written by a Canadian doctor. The lawyer recommended that the college pursue discipline against the pharmacist.

As president, I protested that decision due to the high cost of lawyers' fees on both sides and the fact that no harm was being done to patients.

In the end, the college took the pharmacist to discipline; he was found guilty, and fined. The pharmacist appealed, and the judge overturned the guilty decision and the fine, since there was no intent to harm any patient. The college would have saved the money on legal fees if they had listened to me in the first place!

My biggest accomplishment during my term was to bring the College of Pharmacists of BC together with the College of Dental Surgeons to build our own building, which has saved us thousands of dollars in rental costs throughout the years.

## Nikken and Other Multi-Level-Marketing

In 1975 an inventor in Japan engineered magnetic shoe inserts that massaged sore feet, launching the direct marketing company Nikken. These inserts, named Magsteps, tended to help with all-over body fatigue. After that, the company introduced a massage roller for sore backs and then advanced sleep technology.

I started with Nikken in Vancouver in the early eighties, when there were only four or five people in the business. There were only four of us at the first meeting. I remember Bruce Black of Black's Cameras because he was heavily involved in the company. Nikken had two kinds of products, magnetic and ceramic. They were the first to introduce ceramic products. Ceramics are composed of a type of sand with different kinds of metal oxides. Changing the formula of the ceramics increased its reflective qualities, just as the tiles on the space shuttle can reflect heat.

Nikken discovered a certain formula of rare oxides that would reflect the body's infrared energy back into the body. They would grind the ceramic very, very finely and capture it inside a polymer thread, which reflected the infrared energy. It would actually raise the vibration of the molecules in blood vessels, causing them to open up, resulting in better circulation and pain reduction.

I did very well with Nikken. I won a trip to Japan as one of the top salespeople in Vancouver, attending a huge convention of about forty to fifty thousand people. We took a tour of Nikken headquarters and had time to sightsee around Tokyo and other historic sites in Japan.

When I heard I had won, I was really excited. I had never been to Japan and I had no idea I would become one of the top producers. I was very surprised.

There were people there from all over the world, not just Canadians and Americans. It was a big company and they did very well for a while. Like all multilevel marketing enterprises, they had their high spots and their lows, their very good years and their lulls.

Japan was quite expensive. A cup of coffee in downtown Tokyo would set you back fifteen dollars. You could eat very cheaply if you ate the local food. It became costly ordering American or Canadian food. For a steak dinner, you'd have to spend fifty bucks.

Their streets were so full of pedestrians compared to ours. It was so crowded and busy, with advertisements trying to get your attention. There were lots of little cars and tons and tons of traffic and blinking neon. This was in the eighties; their economy was booming, and it was a great time to visit Japan.

## The Advent of ThermoFlow

One day a flyer was dropped off at the pharmacy promoting products similar to Nikken's. I started selling these products, called ThermoFlow Far Infrared, because they were much cheaper. A Nikken knee wrap cost about forty-five dollars, and this company's wrap was fifteen. It turns out I was the only one in the area selling ThermoFlow. The lady who owned the company came to the pharmacy and asked if I would become the sole distributor. I thought since I was buying them myself, I would definitely be able to sell them.

We took advantage of the expertise of Jay Abraham's marketing courses in Los Angeles. He put together five thousand dollars per-person lectures with hundreds of people in the room, covering how to get free promotion and the best places to advertise, giving tips on marketing skills and valuable up-to-date information. He came up with the logo for ThemoFlow and the slogan "Pain Care You Wear," as well as "If the Pain Doesn't Go Away, You Don't Have to Pay." It helped that we had a money-back guarantee. We would send Jay our marketing material and he would go over it and give us great ideas and suggestions.

## Radio Host

I advertised ThermoFlow on the radio, and eventually got my own talk show, which became one of my biggest sales mechanisms. It all started when my pharmacist employee and I attended the BC Home and Garden Show and met a female radio host. We had to pay to be on her show, but we did very well. Eventually, we decided we could do that ourselves and we got our own time slot.

We would spend one segment talking about Thermo-Flow and the other ten- to fifteen-minute segments speaking about other products. We called the show "Natural Health Solutions." Sometimes the shows were live and other times taped. We would take calls from listeners, depending on the product. Our goal was to make the time interesting, informative, and controversial.

Once we got used to being on the radio, it was very simple. We knew the products we were talking about. We would line up people to call in with testimonials and questions. We seemed to appeal to enough listeners, because they didn't kick us off the air and we did it for about twelve years! People still comment to me about hearing me on the radio, even though I'm not on the air anymore.

A radio station that specialized in women's talk shows ran our show, as did another station called CKNW—the number one talk show station in the Vancouver area—so we reached a wide audience. CKNW actually called us one Thursday because someone had cancelled and they had a one-hour slot available. My other pharmacist and I went down to the station that Saturday and performed the show. We ended up selling about thirty thousand dollars' worth of products in one week just from that single show. Normally we earned five to ten thousand dollars per show at the other radio station, but this one had a much larger audience. We were averaging about sixty thousand dollars a month out of a thousand-foot store with vitamins, ThermoFlow, and other natural products.

I built up the ThermoFlow sales to thirty thousand dollars out of my one store. I was selling to about eighty other stores as well. We still have pretty good sales—over ten thousand dollars a month, advertised with thirty-second radio ads now.

I've always been a big user of natural products. I take vitamins and some of the other products we sell as well. We got into some trouble with the College of Pharmacists. They didn't think it was right for pharmacists to promote natural products. They never shut us down; they would just send us little warnings once in a while. They thought we were going too close to the edge.

I sold ThermoFlow for about fifteen years, and around 2009 the woman who owned the company decided she was going to retire, so I bought the company. I still own it. My brother-in-law, Mel, runs it for me full-time now, out of the warehouse in Richmond.

We still do radio commercials but I don't have a show anymore. We advertise on the station that covers sports and all the hockey games. A lot of men buy these products for their old sports injuries, for arthritis, fibromyalgia, and back strain. They're also good for hand strain from using Black-Berrys, smart phones, and gaming. We have special gloves for thumb pain. There really is a product to help everyone.

## Noni Juice and More

Through the years I tried a lot of multilevel marketing products (MLMs). I sold Tahitian noni juice. I was one of the first to sell this juice and I still drink it. I have signed up enough people under me to get my own product for free, but I don't promote it much anymore. I used to sell two to three hundred cases per month.

The noni company actually shut me down once because I promoted it on the radio. I sold two hundred cases overnight. They told me I couldn't sell it on the radio without prior approval because they were afraid I would steal all the sales in the area. There was no way I could get preapproved for content, because we never knew what we would talk about on the show word for word.

I have pretty good instincts about which products will work and which won't. I follow my hunches. There are some products I thought would work and didn't, and others that I didn't think would work at all and they took off. But some products I just knew from the very beginning would be successful. I get calls offering me new MLM products every day. I know thousands of people in the multilevel marketing industry.

People in that industry move around all the time, but they move as a group. As an MLM starts to be less profitable, and industry people see another one starting to rise, they'll go to the next company and bring their whole organization with them. In this business you can build your own success because you are the company and you keep your followers.

Multilevels are very interesting that way; they become their own drivers. You get the right people behind you, and before you know it, what you're promoting just starts to grow. I didn't actually move en masse with people. There were certain people I could trust who knew more about multilevels than I did. When I got a call from this type of person, I could tell they were onto something. They wouldn't move from the very high end of one company to another without knowing it was a good investment.

One of the products I tried for a bit featured Muhammad Ali as a spokesperson. It was a vegetarian hamburger. It was short-lived, but I met a lot of good businesspeople. I still get a kick out of the picture I have of me with Muhammad Ali, "The Greatest."

I was in multilevels for years juggling many balls in the air at once. I had a lot of energy and I knew the right people to call. Knowing the right people and not wasting time with the wrong people is crucial in that line of work.

Sheldon thinks the reason I was so entrepreneurial was because it felt good to me to be successful at a lot of things. He didn't think it was all about the money for me—and I have to agree with him. I was more excited about meeting Ali than the potential for profit from any product.

Once Sheldon and I bought a warehouse together and I was managing it when Sheldon was living up north. We'd agreed to split the income. I was supposed to rent out the upper space but I was letting some guy down on his luck use the space until he got on his feet. I suppose I had a soft spot for helping people in need. Sheldon sure thinks I did because I'd do things like that and not worry about losing money. There was a methadone clinic down the street from my pharmacy, and one day a strung-out guy stumbled in. Sheldon and I were having a conversation at the counter and he spotted this guy shoplifting a chocolate bar and pointed it out. I felt sorry for the guy and told Sheldon, "That guy probably just needs his sugar." I let it go.

I believe this trait came from my dad. When we visited family in the summertime in Winnipeg, my father used to work with my uncle harvesting the grain on the farm. When he could have been relaxing, my dad was doing those types of things. We both had the same gene for helping out other people.

## Internet Pharmacy

For a while the Internet pharmacy was highly lucrative. Many Americans wanted to buy their prescription drugs from Canada because they were so much cheaper. You'd advertise by buying words online, bidding on each word in the Internet ad at two or three cents per click. It was crazy and exhilarating and frustrating at the same time. The stakes were always rising—it was almost like gambling. Pretty soon the per-click price would go way up. Lipitor actually went to five dollars per click.

We were able to build our Internet pharmacy to huge numbers, hundreds of thousands of dollars a month. But it was short-lived. There were only four years that the Canadian dollar was really weak and the American dollar had more purchasing power. That was in the nineties.

I had a stroke of insight and went down to the US to buy advertising on the Frank Sinatra Hour for our Internet pharmacy Web site. That was a huge success—we received thousands and thousands of hits and it was really cheap advertising. It wasn't prime time, but the right kind of people were listening—the correct age group for our products.

The drug companies pulled all sorts of dirty tricks on us. They went to Visa and MasterCard to try to convince them not to accept online pharmacy purchases. We had to keep changing our company names to keep our accounts.

We'd receive letters at the pharmacy saying that we could no longer buy Lipitor. So we would have to open all new online stores just to get Lipitor, then purchase Lipitor off that account until they figured it out and shut that account down, then we'd go open another account under a new name.

I believe drugs do have their advantages, especially if we think about what has happened in the last twenty or thirty years. When was the last time anyone had an operation for an ulcer? In the old days if you had a stomach ulcer, it would have to be removed in a hospital. Nowadays you take a drug for it, and it's gone.

Drugs can do a lot of good, but sometimes Big Pharma has too much power, and they abuse that power. Drug makers can develop a drug that's very effective and doing well, and then block other companies from getting into that market. They may also publish their own clinical studies swaying or massaging data one way or the other. You can't believe everything those companies are putting out there. It pays to be very careful and discerning with the drug companies, and to be vigilant with your own health and well-being.

## Chapter Eleven

## My Love for Travel

B arb and I have always done a lot of traveling together. One of my favourite places we went to before we had kids was San Francisco. We went there to visit some friends. I loved it. It reminded me of Vancouver. It has stunning views, the excitement of the waterfront shops with great seafood, the clanging trolleys, and Chinatown.

After our kids were born, we went on many family trips and, just like our parents did, we took the kids out of school more than their teachers would have liked, but the family time and memories we made were important to us. I could take time off when I wanted to since I was self-employed, and Barb had four weeks' holiday every year when she worked as a nurse. She worked part time for a long time, but when Craig was born, she quit working. Then we could take off whenever we wanted when school was in session so it wasn't as crowded at our destinations.

As the kids grew older we wanted to travel with them and show them some of the world beyond their borders. Costa Rica was our first big trip. I met a guy at one of the trade and travel shows in Vancouver and he was able to find us a great place, a house built around a large pool. It was a beautiful pool, with part of it covered with a thatched roof so when it got too hot everyone could swim in the shade. The boys loved diving for keys in the pool. One time they couldn't find the keys and we all thought they were lost and locked out. They couldn't figure out how that could happen; it was a mystery, but eventually they found them still in the pool. We all loved seeing the volcano (from afar) and driving in the tall, skinny, funny-looking van. There was a black sand beach to stroll on down below us as well, on the Pacific Ocean.

In Costa Rica there were really big insects. We were all freaked out by a huge cockroach sitting by our table in a little restaurant that we stopped in, though none of the other patrons seemed to mind. We wended our way through the rainforest along the walkways and took in all sorts of trees, plants, and wonderful flowers. We hiked around near a volcano that erupts a little bit all the time, every day. When you hike up the mountain and gaze across to the volcano, there's a sign that says, "If Volcano Explodes Leave Area Immediately!" We all got a big chuckle out of that.

At one point, when we were exploring in our little blue van, we approached a river and the road stopped and picked up again on the other side. I wasn't sure what to do, so I backed the van away and waited for a while. Sure enough, another car came along, drove right through the river and kept on going. I figured if he could do it, I could do it. It was about thirty feet across, but who knew what was in the middle? I don't know if it was a high water level that year or if people were just driving through this river all the time as if it were a normal thing. But we did it—and we got to the other side.

In Costa Rica there were potholes as big as cars. You'd be driving along and all of a sudden the road was washed out with this gigantic hole in the middle. No sensible person would ever want to drive at night. You'd be driving along and boom—you'd fall into a pit and wreck your car.

One night we went on a sailboat ride at sunset, watching the sky turn colours as we glided through the water. The trip was mostly about enjoying the pool and doing a little snorkelling. It was so relaxing. The kids enjoyed the pool and the volcano the most.

Because I had such an eye-opening experience in Europe, I wanted to share that with my kids, so our next international vacation was to England, Scotland and France. This was a tall order, as the size of our family dictated how we were going to take in the sights from country to country. The smallest vehicle we could find in London to fit everyone was called a Transit, which we needed because we had four kids. It was one of those contraptions they use to pick people up at the airport. They had plenty of cars for four or five people but none for six, and the Transit held twelve! So what could we do except rent it and put our luggage on the extra seats.

I had to drive this thing all the way around England through tiny, narrow streets, on the "wrong" side of the road. My family loved it though. We took them to all the castles and tried to take advantage of all the outdoor sites and festivals we could. We hiked quite a bit and my kids loved spotting so many fortresses, spires, and manor houses as we drove and exploring the cathedrals, synagogues, and museums. We had some bad luck in Manchester, when our van was broken into and the thieves stole our British souvenirs and all of Alisa's CDs.

Of course when travelling in Europe, we had some sunny days and some rainy days. In Edinburgh it was pouring and cold. That's the way the weather often is in the UK. We didn't stay in the north very long because it was so chilly and damp. We loved seeing the castles in the countryside, and we spent a few days in London enjoying all the museums and Hyde Park. The British Museum is absolutely huge and filled with archaeology, history, statues, and art. Half of the remains of Greek and Roman temples are in the British Museum—it was just fascinating.

I remember a terrifying exhibit on torture devices in the Tower of London. They would place manacles on a dummy convict's wrists and leave them hanging, and they showed "the rack," which stretched lawbreakers and political dissidents by the arms and legs, popping their joints, tendons, and muscle fibres. There's so much in London to see.

In Paris, we went to the Eiffel Tower, and there was a church with three to four hundred stairs that the kids wanted to climb to the top. My wife and I said we'd wait for them and just have a nice cup of coffee. We enjoyed the break, but the coffee and hot chocolate cost us fifteen dollars. We were shocked at how high the prices were compared to back home, and that was in 1996.

Rather than staying in hotels, we spent many of our nights at farms in the countryside that had bed and breakfasts. It was a different experience for the kids seeing the farmers milking cows in the morning, and a more relaxing atmosphere than a motel.

I enjoyed staying at the quaint bed and breakfasts on working farms along the way. The other times we stayed in motels like Travelodges. Because it was so expensive, we couldn't afford two rooms and they only allowed four people per room. We used the same plan that we had on our US road trip, sneaking two kids into the room, and it worked very well!

I asked Kevin and Craig what they remember and they don't recall much about Europe, except being in a lot of castles and the fact that I drove through a roundabout on the wrong side of the road. Kevin was twelve and Craig was only ten. Alisa was seventeen and Jeffrey was fifteen. I think Alisa got the most out of it, especially since she has always been interested in English literature and history.

## Nature Travel

Travel has been a passion of mine ever since I can remember. Canoeing and freshwater fishing are my favourite ways to be in nature. After the disaster with the canoe on our honeymoon, Barb and I stopped in Winnipeg to visit relatives and that's where I bought a Kildonan canoe. It's a special canoe with a balsa wood core, with no need for heavy struts and supports. It is quite light, made for portaging. I still have it in my garage, although I haven't taken it out for a few years.

One of my favourite places to go canoeing and camping was at Bowron Lakes, a one hundred sixteen kilometre chain of multiple lakes and waterways in a rectangular shape. I glided my way through Bowron Lakes twice in a canoe with Ken Garfinkel. He and I also enjoyed some smaller trips of two and three days over on Vancouver Island. Bowron, though, was without a doubt the longest and most amazing canoe trip I've ever been on. It took us about a week to go around all of the lakes with portaging between bodies of water.

The first time we did the Bowron system, it had rained heavily the previous week and the trail was a mess. The initial three portages were done through calf-high mud. The two of us dragged the food and supplies to the first lake, tied the food on a line between two trees, and went back for the canoe. We had to do this twice on the first day and we were so tired that we prayed that the next one hundred kilometres would be easier that the last five!

Once on the lake it was beautiful. When we were tired of paddling we would find a stick on the shore and with the second paddle set up a sail using raincoats. One of us would sit in the back and steer, while the other would lounge in the front. I loved the spectacular scenery. We saw deer, bear, moose, and many other kinds of wildlife almost every day and enjoyed the quiet—no motorboats allowed. It was so quiet we could hear wildlife scurrying through the grasses, fish jumping, and the calls of the birds. The mist would come up on the lake in the morning and the trees would stand out vividly green against the clear blue sky. The mountains came down right into the lake, and there would sometimes be glaciers and patches of icy snow in the crevasses. The sunsets would light up the clouds with oranges and pinks, as the dark outlines of the mountains stood out against the brighter sky.

We could sit there for hours and fish or paddle away, leaving a wake of our own in the green lake, which from a distance looked as blue as the sky. Sometimes we had destinations in mind and other days we would meander, doing whatever suited us, welcoming diversions like detouring into a sandy cove, discovering a waterfall, or watching deer frolicking in a meadow.

Most of the days were slightly chilly, even in August. It just never seemed to warm up in the Cariboo Mountains. Nowadays, the Bowron Lakes are such a coveted destination that boaters need to book a year in advance. The government has laid out selected spots where people are allowed to camp, with ironclad restrictions in place. Certain areas are forbidden because of bears, and all food must to be kept in metal containers.

At one campsite we were awoken by the sounds of people yelling and pots banging just up the lake from us. A bear had wandered into the campsite of another group and was ignoring the clatter. The common method of bear-proofing your food was to tie a rope across two trees and hang the knapsacks down from the rope. This time, the bear climbed up the tree above the rope and jumped down onto the sacks, its claws ripping the knapsacks to pieces, flinging food all over the campsite. The bear bit through a couple of tins and was very pleased to find a large can of peaches that it took to the woods.

On our second trip to Bowron Lakes we had another bear experience. Our cooling system was a styrofoam acid bottle container, hollowed out and shaved to fit under the canoe seat. After a few days on the lakes our cooling system no longer kept things cool and we needed to eat our last steak. With the fire going, we enjoyed steak and eggs for breakfast. While breaking camp, Ken was cleaning the frying pan, when he heard something behind him. It was a bear moving quickly towards him looking for breakfast. The frying pan went straight to the bear's face accompanied with a series of expletives, and a shout to get into the canoe fast. We paddled off shore and watched the bear go through our stuff and then wander off without doing much harm.

Another memorable day on our second trip was when we entered Isaac Lake. We had been told to hug the northern shore because the southern shore rises straight out of the lake and there are no established camping sites or even places to land. Being veterans of the system we felt overly confident and hugged the south shore. It was a beautiful sunny day and we were feeling adventurous. We found a small area to set the canoe and went exploring. Suddenly, we found what looked like gold dust. After all, we were in gold country, near the area of the Cariboo gold rush of the 1860s. So, we panned for gold and dreamed about the riches we would find.

We each had our little poke of gold when we saw a forbidding black cloud at the far side of the lake. We decided to head across to the north side as fast as we could. About half way across the lake, the storm hit with a vengeance. We could not move and we were being swamped in the middle of nowhere. We were pushed back against the south shore, with nowhere to land, and the wind and rain and waves from the lake were smashing us against the mountainside. During what seemed to be our last moments afloat, we spied a small shelf about twenty feet above the lake. Ken managed to climb up with a rope and we hauled our supplies up the rock face. Then, we were able to tie our canoe above us so it hung down and provided us with a bit of shelter. We discussed our predicament and came to the conclusion that we had just upset the gold gods of Isaac Lake. With the storm pounding against our cold, drenched bodies, we decided to show our respect and return the gold. Within half an hour of throwing our gold back, the sun came out and we made the crossing to the north side of the lake. We would have to find another way to make our fortunes!

## Exotic Travel

The most amazing trip Barb and I took together was in 2006, to Tahiti. First, we stayed in a time-share on Mooréa for a week, then we spent two days in an overwater bungalow and then we were off on a Society Islands cruise for a week. I have to say that the overwater bungalow was to die for, a completely extraordinary experience. Our bungalow sat facing out into the water in a circular shape, so there was privacy and a panoramic view all our own. Inside was a glass coffee table with a glass floor below, to view all the colourful fish underneath. If you threw them little bits of bread, hundreds of fish in all different shapes and sizes and colours swam up underneath. It was so beautiful and thrilling to watch.

We had a big deck, and four steps down to the water, another deck. From the lower deck, all you had to do was step into the ocean and you could snorkel with the fish in the clear turquoise water.

At the beginning of our stay in the overwater bungalows, it didn't seem so carefree and effortless. We received a coupon for this resort due to all the air miles we'd accumulated. In French Polynesia most of the people working behind the counters speak French. We were at the counter showing the representative our coupon, and the woman was looking at it as if she'd never seen this type before. I was getting worried because it was a very expensive place and I didn't want to have to pay the full price. She told us she had to make a phone call and left for quite some time. To say I was getting concerned was an understatement. Finally, she emerged from the back office, looked down at me, and said, "It's okay. I've upgraded you to the overwater bungalow." Whew! What a relief! We never did find out why we got so lucky.

Because these structures are built way out over the ocean, we actually drove golf carts over decks to reach our bungalow. That decking went a long, long way. When you're there, you feel like this is how the wealthy live, with all the amenities you'd ever want. There's a flat screen TV in your thatched-roof bungalow, yet you're sitting right over the water.

The resort had its own restaurants, but there were also plenty of superb restaurants in Mooréa with delicious food—mostly European. We went to a Swiss restaurant that was amazing, with different fondues. There were German restaurants and, of course, French restaurants; all different kinds of European food with rich sauces. They didn't give us huge quantities of food, but the food that we were served was quite rich and very delicately made—the carrots were carved in a certain way—quite detail oriented. It was not cheap but very good and worth every penny.

After the bungalow, we embarked on a week-long Princess Cruise on the Tahitian Princess. The snorkelling was a highlight of the cruise, seeing all the exotic fish and the colourful coral underwater. It was like living in a dream you don't want to end.

We found we could enjoy similar food and atmosphere in a subsequent trip to Fiji, where the water is also pure and sparkling, with colourful fish and coral and, of course, balmy warm weather—but the culture was different. Tahiti is more European. In Fiji, the food and the atmosphere were more natural, more native. In Fiji we also went on a cruise, but it was a smaller ship with about three hundred fifty people, with excellent food and service. Barb and I loved both trips to the South Pacific.

## Dipping My Toe in the Travel Business

I loved travel so much that when an opportunity came up for me to make money on tours and travel at the same time, I grabbed it. While working in the pharmacy, I met a missionary who had worked in Thailand and Vietnam when he was younger. He would come in and buy lottery tickets. He convinced me I should work in the travel industry with him.

He'd arrange groups going to Thailand and other places in the Far East. He had been there so many times, he had it down pat. He would put out a notice for a bus trip for fifty-two people and fill it up just like that. I couldn't do that myself since I was busy with the pharmacy, so I needed a partner.

At first he was going to sell his entire business to me. Then he decided he didn't want to sell the name, only the business part of it. Unfortunately, I went along with that, and I learned that the name is everything in travel. He could advertise and lure forty people right off the bat, while I put out an ad and had a hard time getting twenty people.

This man showed us how to run the business, though. We would offer the same tour to Thailand and he would arrange it all for us. All we had to do is run the ads and book it—but that part wasn't so easy. It did give me more opportunity to see different parts of the world, however, and meet many interesting people.

One of the things I was attracted to in Thailand were the marketplaces—thousands of people and all that glorious merchandise in all those little stalls, tiny shops, and bazaars. There was a marketplace that set up only at night with twinkling lights under the stars. I had a good time with the bargaining part, really got a kick out of it. I'm the only one in my family who enjoys that. It makes some people nervous. But many people in these countries speak enough English to get by. You can stick up your fingers and find other ways to show them how much money you're willing to spend.

There were so many sights to see; the ruins of holy temples were really amazing. When you go to any of these ancient ruins there's a special energy around them because they've seen so much history and have so many stories to tell. They've been around so long you can't help thinking about what went on during ancient times. Here in North America a building doesn't often last more than thirty or forty years before they tear it down. There is so much history in Thailand.

I arranged one trip to Singapore and Thailand and one group that went to Singapore, Thailand, and Malaysia. Another group toured Greece and Turkey. None of them were profitable. We lost money on the venture and we closed up. It was a learning experience, and I did get to visit places I hadn't been before and probably wouldn't have gone to. I also learned a lot about travel and different tricks of the trade.

## Chapter Twelve

# Mom's Good-bye

All through our lives my mother was a constant presence. She helped out in my store, she had us over for delicious meals, and she looked after our kids—not only when she was babysitting, but when they needed her advice, and then she was always reachable by phone. Well into old age, my mother had endless energy and she loved being around people. She was a real people person.

My mother would take care of the children when my wife and I would go on holiday. Alisa says my mother was always very concerned about them. She would ask, "Did you have enough to eat? Aren't you going to be cold without a jacket? Don't cross any busy streets!" She was very protective.

She would do everything for them that Barb thought they were old enough to do for themselves, such as fix their own breakfast, make lunch for school, and do their own laundry. It was a vacation for our kids too when we were away!

My mother loved being around family and having a full house. Whenever she'd have us over for dinner on Sundays she would make brisket and rice, putting mushroom soup in the rice to give it a much better flavour. The recipe now has an honoured place in our family—it's called "Bubby's Rice."

When Alisa was angry with us, my mother was the one she would call. She would always listen to Alisa and make her feel better. My mother was the one who took our kids back-to-school shopping, and when they were growing out of their clothes, she'd buy them a whole new wardrobe. She loved being at the mall.

My friends talk about visiting their elderly parents. Well, we couldn't visit my mother very much because she was never home. You'd have to make an appointment to see her. She would meet her friends every day at the mall and hang out in the food court, until the time came when she had to move into a retirement home because she had a few falls and we were getting worried about her living on her own.

Sheldon, Bonnie, and I all talked about moving her into a retirement home where she could be cared for and looked after, and we decided it was the best and safest option. On one hand it was probably a mistake because where she lived was only about a block from the shopping centre. The food court was her social centre. She'd be over there twice a day having coffee or lunch with her friends. When she moved into the retirement home there was no encouragement for her to get out and walk somewhere. She would say, "The senior centre is for old people," and she was serious. She was in her eighties when she said that.

She was pretty upset about not being able to walk across the street to Oakridge mall anymore, even though she had lots of friends in her retirement home. It wasn't long after that she started getting dizzy spells and going to the doctor more often. Then my sister phoned and said my mom was going to the hospital because she was dizzy and short of breath, so we all went to the hospital to see her.

They did some tests and found there was a blockage in her heart and she couldn't get enough air. They tried to put a stent into her heart, but this was unsuccessful, and she died a few hours later. Literally within seven or eight hours, she was gone. It was devastating. It was a shock for me, and all of my kids. They were so used to her being there. She died in November of 2009. She was eighty-six. It was hard for everyone, but at least her three children and many of her grandchildren were there at the hospital to see her before she died. We all miss her every day.

# Chapter Thirteen

## To Sum It Up . . .

Barb and I went back to Cornwall in 2009. It still looked exactly the same to me; the streets and old buildings had not changed a bit from when I grew up. It's still pretty quiet, unlike Vancouver, where they are always demolishing one thing and building something else, and things never stay the same.

The federal government tried to get a pilot school going there, but it still hasn't done much for the economy. Cornwall has one of the highest unemployment rates of any city in Canada. They've attempted many programs but they haven't been successful.

I've told the kids many stories of how it was to grow up there; it's so far from what they experienced in Vancouver. In Cornwall, the wintertime was snowy and cold and the power would often go out, and with it, the heat. Once the snow had finally melted, the spring was so welcome after all that cold, and the summers were muggy and hot. It's much drier than on the West Coast. After looking around at the houses and how industry had taken hold of the land, river, and the air, we were grateful to have had our children grow up where they did, in our very own house we built in Richmond.

In my life, family has been a priority for me. I've always been interested in learning about my family history, and I've created a huge family tree using a computer program. I got my start as an entrepreneur with the help of my uncles, and I've employed multiple family members in my store and my businesses. I also gave my son Jeff the start of his career. Alisa says I do everything I can to provide for us, just as my family members, like my dad, Uncle Harry, and Uncle Harvey, did for me.

Even though we're not a family that talks about feelings or is overly affectionate, we are very close in terms of time spent together, helping each other out, and trying to stay together proximally. And though my brother and sister have each lived in different parts of Canada, they both came back to Vancouver, and my children all live close by. Even Kevin, in Seattle, is only a few hours away. We've done family trips to Whistler and Salt Spring Island with all of the kids and grandkids, and I love having pictures taken with all my grandkids together.

I've always been interested in travel and new technology. In my life, I've done many things more for the excitement, the fun of investing in new possibilities. This philosophy may not work for other people, but it's worked for me. My motto was: "Follow the dream and the money will follow."

I don't always plan out the financial aspect down to the very nickel (how many people do I need to recruit to do this, what do I need to make that profitable?), I just set it up and hope it runs. A lot of people are risk-averse; they just don't want to take chances in their lives. That's never been my interest at all. I have to be active and challenged.

Today, it's hard to believe I've grown from such an introverted boy with a rather inauspicious start in Cornwall, Ontario, to someone who knows thousands of people, has been a radio host, Internet marketer, and has travelled the world. I owe this to saying yes to so many possibilities, from pursuing my future wife to plunging ahead in new adventures and industries.

The main insight I can take from my past is that I grabbed at opportunities and I just took them. A lot of things present themselves and other people let them float on by. I have even let a few things slide by myself. But every once in a while, you see a promising venture and you just catch hold of it, and even though it seems insurmountable at first, you just go with it. It's happened to me a few times in my life that chances came up and I just grabbed at them and they worked out.

I was involved in a group where they told us we should map out our future and make a five-year plan, and have a plan for this and a plan for that. That works for some people, but I think your best successes often happen without planning. People tend to overanalyze everything. If something comes up that gives you a good feeling and it makes sense, with a little faith and courage, it can really change your life.

I've been blessed with a strong and varied career, a loving wife and family, and the ability to chart my own course, and I've had a great life. If I had to give advice to my friends, my family, or anyone else, I'd tell them: "Do what you feel like doing when you feel like doing it. And don't put off till tomorrow, because sometimes tomorrow doesn't come!"

In 2012, I found out I had pancreatic cancer and I've been receiving chemo and radiation, as well as taking supplements to stay as healthy as possible in the time that I have left.

I had a surgery to remove the cancer, but it was unsuccessful, as the cancer had spread. At my big sixty-fifth birthday party in October of 2013, I was surprised and very touched by all the friends and relatives who showed up. Even my best friend, Ron Pearson, travelled all the way from the Yukon to come and see me. They all made a big deal of showing that they loved me and that they cared. I never imagined so many people would turn out to celebrate with me.

I always thought I'd die of a heart attack, given my family history, so the cancer has been a shock for me and everyone else. I have sold all of my businesses, and the one that was most profitable was the sale of the nursing home business, where my son Jeff still works.

I'd like to be remembered as a loving husband, father, and grandfather. I feel devastated to know that my life is coming to an end. I'm going to miss seeing my grandkids grow up and celebrate their Bar and Bat Mitzvahs when they turn thirteen. I would have liked being around for at least ten more years.

I want to spend my final days surrounded by my wife and family, and I'm comforted by the idea that I will be able to see my mother, father, and little sister again in the next world. I can see my father so clearly now, even though he's been a long time gone. For right now, I'm enjoying being with my wife and kids, and the hugs and kisses I'm receiving from the grandchildren, reading books to them while they sit on my lap.

Marvin Nider

October 12, 1948 — March 13, 2014

Sarah and Oscar (on right) – 1950s –
out to dinner with friends

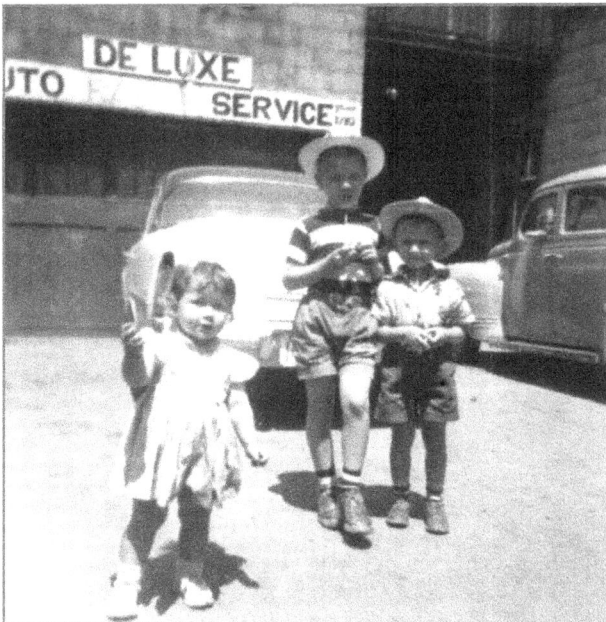

Sandra, Sheldon, Marvin – circa 1954 –
taken in front of Oscar's auto repair garage

Marvin, Sheldon, Sarah, Sandra – 1955 – family portrait

Sandra, Sheldon, Marvin, family dog (Rinny) – 1956 –
sitting in the backyard of the house Oscar built

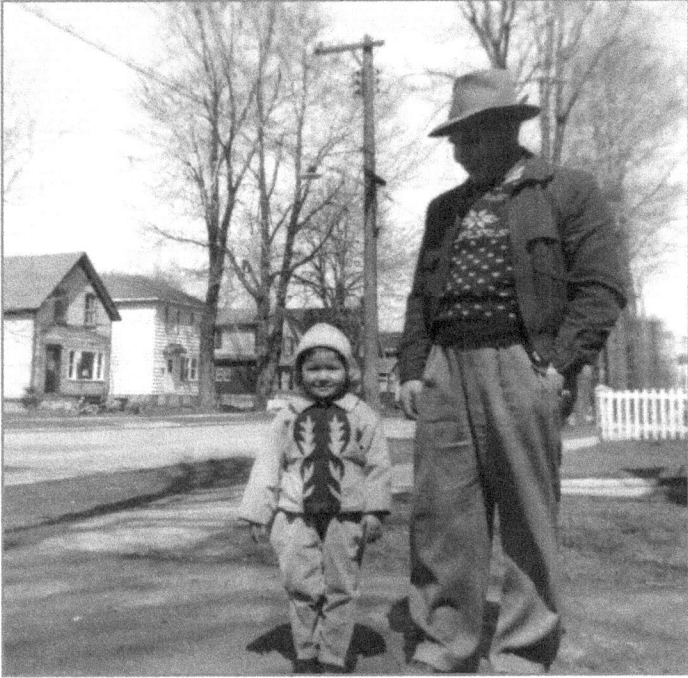

Sandra and Oscar – 1956 –
standing on the street near their house

Oscar Niduvitch – circa 1960 –
standing beside his driving school vehicle

Sheldon, Bonnie, Marvin – 1961 –
taken in Cornwall on the day of Marvin's Bar Mitzvah

Bonnie - 1961 –
four years old

Bonnie, Marvin – Circa 1967 –
Bonnie and Marvin posing

Ken Waldman, Marvin, Ken Garfinkel, Peter Kafka – 1970 –
before their trip to Europe,
photo taken at Vancouver Airport

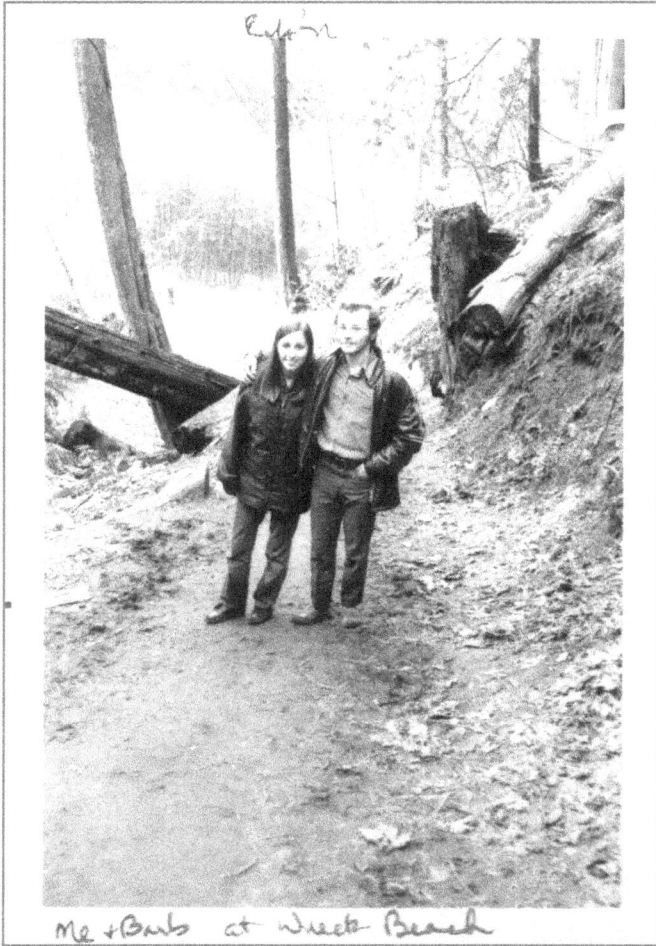

Barb, Marvin – early 1970's –
standing on the path to Wreck Beach at UBC

Marvin – 1974 – canoeing at Bowron Lakes

Ken, Marvin – 1974 –
pictured at Bowron Lakes

Bonnie, Sarah, Marvin, Sheldon – May 23, 1976 –
Barb and Marvin's wedding day

Marvin and Barb – May 23, 1976 –
at Queen Elizabeth Park

Marvin, Jeffrey, Craig, Alisa, Barb, Kevin – 1992 –
family trip to Disney World

Barb and Marvin – January 2006 –
trip to Tahiti

Marvin, Barb – January 2006 –
pictured in a restaurant in Tahiti

Family trip to Salt Spring Island – August 2013
(back row) Craig, Marvin, Barb, Kevin, Robin
(middle row) Marc, Jeff, Elizabeth, Daniel, Alisa
(front row) Aviva, Sari, Ephraim, Yosef, Zoey

www.ingramcontent.com/pod-product-compliance
Lightning Source LLC
Chambersburg PA
CBHW060544100426

42742CB00013B/2445